THE STR
OF BUSI....

A STUDENT'S HANDBOOK

M. M. LAWTON
J. MAGUIRE

General Editor: J. R. M. ASLETT

HULTON EDUCATIONAL

FOREWORD

This book is intended to be a guide for those taking Business Studies and others who are interested in the workings of the business world. After reading *The Structure of Business* they should, therefore, refer also to recent textbooks which deal with each subject in detail.

It should be particularly emphasised that, because conditions are continually changing, students must keep up-to-date by reading newspapers, bank reviews, government publications and other current material.

ACKNOWLEDGEMENTS

My thanks are due to members of the government departments mentioned in the text for their help in providing information and to my family and friends for their patience and help. I am indebted to Mr J. Aslett for his valuable assistance and guidance. It is as a result of his instigation and persuasion that this book has been written. M. M. L.

In the revision of this work, many educationalists have given helpful comment, officials of the departments have supplied valuable updated material and, above all, Mr J. Aslett has co-operated with his expert guidance. For all this, I record grateful appreciation.   J. M.

First published in Great Britain 1972
by Hulton Educational Publications Ltd
Old Station Drive, Leckhampton
Cheltenham GL53 0DN

Revised and reprinted 1975; reprinted 1977
Second edition 1980; reprinted 1982
Third edition 1984 (completely reset with
revisions and updated information); reprinted 1986 (twice)

ISBN 0 7175 1243 6

Printed in Great Britain by Ebenezer Baylis and Son, Worcester

GENERAL EDITOR'S PREFACE

The need for a further edition of this book has provided an opportunity to revise some of the details of economic and governmental changes, and to adjust to the London Chamber of Commerce and Industry's amended syllabus for the Private Secretary's Certificate.

The new syllabus has less emphasis on certain aspects of human relations and on the detailed study of government departments at work. These topics have been revised, but nevertheless kept, partly because they are needed for the Secretarial Studies Certificate and other examinations for which the book has proved useful, but mostly because they are seen as contributory to the fullest understanding of the remaining required studies.

The book has retained its conventional style. Secretaries are by nature a literate body; their stock-in-trade is words and they take their meaning better than most. Also the authors have always recognised the importance of good teachers in this subject, for it is they who maintain its freshness and who challenge the student to observe current reality and judge what is significant.

For example, change is a fact of modern living. Its impact comes not only from new technology and new materials but from its corrosive effect on existing organisations, values and expectations. On the one hand it destroys and on the other it creates opportunity, but the victims of one are not always the beneficiaries of the other. Often the speed of change exceeds the human ability to absorb it psychologically or emotionally. The latest innovations become outmoded before people can come to terms with them.

Authors must beware of trying to fix such volatile developments too precisely to paper. Today's text and diagrams can too easily look like yesterday's ideas in tomorrow's world.

Hence our belief in good teaching, and the hope that this book, which has proved so useful for many years, will continue to play its part in meeting the needs of students and teachers of these subjects.

J. R. M. ASLETT

PART I

THE BUSINESS ENVIRONMENT

1

THE MIXED ECONOMY

Wealth

The wealth of any country depends upon the amount of natural resources or factors of production it possesses and the way in which it uses them. Just as a man who inherits wealth can spend it unwisely and become poor, so can a country be rich in raw materials and have a low standard of living for its people.

Before any goods can be made, four factors of production are necessary. Land is required on which to build premises in which to work; the raw materials procured from the land are necessary to make the product and provide a source of power. Labour is then needed to extract and process these raw materials and to construct buildings and machines. Capital, in the form of money, premises, machines and other equipment used to produce the goods is also necessary. Given these factors, a fourth one—namely organisation or enterprise—is vital to co-ordinate and manage the other three in the most useful, economic, convenient and satisfactory way. Organisation is essential to ensure progress. It is necessary in the small firm as well as the large, for local authorities as well as nationalised industries, and for every country as a whole as much as for the organisations within it.

In the following chapters we shall be looking at the various forms of organisation in the business world and the contribution each one makes.

The total wealth of any country is known as the national income. This figure is composed either by adding together the value of all goods and services, by totalling all incomes, or by adding together all items of expenditure for any given period.

Britain's national income is calculated each year and the figures published by the government in the Blue Book on National Income and Expenditure. In 1981 the national income was £181,179 m. for the United Kingdom.

This figure is the first determinant of individual wealth, for if this is not high per head of population then the standard of living of the people cannot be high; but just as the way in which one spends one's income helps to decide one's standard of living, so the way in which the national income is allocated or spent determines the general standard of living within a country. National income is examined in Chapter 2, but already it can be seen that management and control of the economy by the government is very important.

Government intervention

It is because of this need and the increasing complexity of the economy that this century has seen increasing intervention by governments. Necessity has forced them to take more and more responsibility for the general performance of the economy and to move away from the laissez-faire (leave well alone) policy of the Industrial Revolution. This century has been scarred by two world wars which retarded Britain's progress in securing foreign markets. Other countries became industrialised, so that Britain not only lost markets but gained increasing competition at a time when the economy was at a low ebb, owing to the heavy cost of war. After the Labour government was elected to power in 1945, it introduced a policy of nationalisation or state control of many basic industries, partly for economic and partly for political reasons. Today there is still a mixture of public and private enterprise, i.e. some industries, such as coal and atomic energy, are owned and controlled by the state and others by private individuals. This is termed a mixed economy. In the following chapters both private and public sectors are examined, and account is taken of recent and proposed changes.

2 ———————————————————————

ECONOMIC POLICY

Management of the economy

Whilst steady economic growth is an important goal, it is only one aim to be pursued in the management of an economy. Other aims must include full or high levels of employment, a strong balance of payments and stability in the value of money (purchasing power). Further aims could be added to this list: indeed, as time goes on, it would seem that the number of ideals an economy should try to achieve increases as do the difficulties which prevent their being met. World conditions are continuously changing, so that what is learned from one set of problems at one time does not provide an answer to similar ones at a later date. The order of priority given to the aims of economic policy is often altered because of changing conditions as well as politics.

Inherent in achieving the aims of economic policy are many other important factors, which affect everyone to some extent. As we have already seen, steady growth of gross national product is necessary if a nation is to have rising living standards; but if the majority of the nation is to benefit, rather than just a few sections of it, regard must be given to this in taxation policies, regional employment policies and others. Similarly, economic growth is increased by a healthy balance of payments which, in turn, implies that reserves are strong and a stable exchange rate is maintained. In short, no economic goal can be pursued independently from the others or, indeed be free from other influences continually at work. In addition, since we are part of a world economy, the activities of one country affect and are affected by those of other countries. This is particularly true of nations like Britain which are dependent on foreign trade for food and raw materials.

From the end of the Second World War to the beginning of the 1970s Britain had rising production, unemployment was low at an average level of 2 per cent and gross national product was increasing at an annual rate of two to three per cent, which was less than the growth of the economies of most other European countries. The other main characteristic of the period was balance of payments problems. One of the main causes of this was heavy demand for goods at home,

10

which led to rises in imports. Exports and invisible earnings did not rise sufficiently, thereby causing considerable deficits in many years. Consequently, the main aims of economic policy from 1945 to 1970 were to increase economic growth and improve the balance of payments. Various income policies were introduced by governments of both the main political parties to reduce the increase in demand at home and restrain rises in incomes and prices. Devaluation of the pound from $2.80 to $2.40 in 1967 helped to improve the balance of payments. That and other factors led to an increase in exports and consequently a record surplus on current account in 1971. (Surplus of earnings from all forms of foreign trade over payments for all forms of goods and services received from abroad.)

By 1973, gross national product was increasing at 5 per cent annually, but unemployment was now rising and inflation was a problem. The impact of the world oil crisis aggravated both problems and reduced economic growth. The energy shortage obviously led to large increases in the cost of oil and rapid inflation, causing a world recession. The effect in Britain was a considerable fall in the output of manufacturing industries, reduced exports, rising inflation and unemployment and a substantial reduction in economic growth.

Control of the economy was now a very difficult task, with inflation and unemployment rising together. This was compounded by the fact that other countries were also suffering from recession which made it more difficult to improve the balance of payments by increasing exports. Limits on pay and price controls already in force were strengthened. The government supported these efforts to control inflation by reducing borrowing by the public sector and generally taking strict control of the money supply. This was done to make certain that resources were available to meet the needs of industry, and not advanced to other sections such as public enterprise, thereby encouraging an increase in production and employment. It also attempted to ensure that industry was able to meet demands for exports as world trading conditions improved. The economy did show some improvement following these measures, but inflation and unemployment have remained problems.

In 1980, the government introduced the 'medium-term strategy', which aimed to control inflation by monetary measures by reducing the money supply. It did this by cutting public expenditure (the spending of local authorities, government departments, nationalised industries, etc.) reducing government borrowing, imposing and encouraging high rates of interest to reduce the demand for money, and generally controlling the amount of money in the economy. Taxation measures were used to support this policy.

The main point to emerge from the above picture is that no economic goal is independent: economic growth, control of unemployment, control of inflation and the achievement of a good balance of payments position are all interrelated and hence, measures taken to achieve any one of these aims affects the others too. The economic performance of other countries, though beyond Britain's control, can have a serious effect on the British economy. The recession in the United States and decline in the value of the dollar obviously affected considerably the economic activity of many countries, because of the dollar's large involvement in world trade. Similarly, the energy crisis has had serious impact on Britain's economy and those of other countries. The effect on Britain has been cushioned by the production of North Sea oil which, in turn, has become more valuable as world demand for energy increases and supply is reduced.

Inflation

The control of rising prices and the depreciating value of money has been an aim of economic policy for many years. In the past, it was thought that the control of inflation created unemployment and that inflation only occurred at times of full or near-full employment. In recent years, the problem has been much more serious because rising inflation has been accompanied by high levels of unemployment.

A simple description of inflation is too much money chasing too few goods. It poses a serious problem because it has so many bad effects. The first obvious one is that one's money buys less and less as prices of goods and services continue to rise and one's standard of living falls as a result. This is made worse by the fact that people on low and fixed incomes, for example pensioners, are most seriously affected and they are the least able to help themselves. As prices rise, those in employment press for higher wages which, unless offset by higher productivity and therefore increased production, add to the cost of goods and services, thereby increasing prices further. These increases apply to goods for export as well as those consumed at home, which means that they are less attractive to people abroad unless rates of inflation in other countries are equally high as, or higher than, those in the exporting country. The resulting fall in exports obviously means a reduction in income from abroad, which causes a balance of payments problem and adds further to the rate of inflation. The balance of payments situation can be made worse by foreign goods being cheaper not only abroad, but also at home, thereby increasing imports while exports are falling. A deficit is created which adds more inflation, reduces economic growth and generally adds to the spiral already existing.

Demands for higher wages are most successful when made by those who belong to strong unions and can exercise power. This leads to unfair distribution of income, and problems of how to decide what any particular job is worth. Often those who provide essential services in the public sector receive a very poor deal because they wish to help the community and have poor bargaining power. Nurses are an example. People who borrow money gain, since their repayments become less in real terms as the value of money falls. Consequently, saving is discouraged. If, as often happens, the rate of interest is increased to encourage people to save, costs are increased and stimulate inflation even further.

It is argued by some economists that some inflation is good for the economy, since deflation leads to unemployment and depression, but clearly, a high level of inflation is injurious and makes economic progress difficult, if not impossible. Successive governments, therefore, introduce policies which are designed to control inflation. These fall into two groups. The first aims to decrease demand for goods and services. It includes increases in taxation, restriction of credit, and raising of interest rates, all of which reduce consumers' spending power (demand). These measures are usually supported by reduced government expenditure which, in turn, decreases the amount of money circulating in the economy and is therefore a further control on demand.

The second group of measures aims to hold or reduce costs and therefore prices. The chief measure is the carrying out of an incomes policy designed to control wages and salaries at a specified level or specific ones to the level of increased productivity achieved. Cost inflation arises when the rise in costs is greater than the rise in output. Control of prices by the government has accompanied recent income policies in Britain. Clearly, however, interest rates increased to curb demand will add to the costs of production, while increases in taxation can increase pressure for higher wages. Economists talk of, and distinguish between, cost-push inflation—price rises which occur because the costs of production are increasing more than output, and demand-pull inflation—price rises which occur as a result of increased demand. The two types of inflation are closely connected. It is obvious that where there is widespread inflation, demands will be made for rises in income to compensate for lack of purchasing power. These increases, assuming they are not accompanied by at least equal rises in productivity, will be spent on goods and services and add to total demand. The result will be further rises in prices which will add to the inflationary spiral. In short, the two types are usually at work together, each perpetuating the inflationary climate.

Control of inflation

In recent years many measures have been used in an attempt to control inflation. The main ones have been those which limit rises in incomes and prices. During the 1960s, there was a formal prices and incomes policy under which government approval had to be obtained through the National Board for Prices and Incomes for any increase in prices or incomes. The 1970s saw a change to voluntary control through the Social Contract between the government and trade unions. The unions agreed to keep wage increases within the guidelines laid down, while the government controlled prices and promised a wide range of social and economic policies, such as the payment of subsidies on certain basic foods, to keep their prices down and the payment of higher social security benefits including pensions. These policies did achieve some success, although the average level of wage increases was double the 5 per cent target originally set.

While prices and incomes policies do help to control inflation, they obviously do not provide a complete answer. The level of prices at home depends to some extent on the prices of imports, which are determined by factors outside our control, as well as on the value of sterling, which depends partly on the levels of other countries' currencies. These are complications which make it difficult for governments to have effective control of prices. Often when prices and incomes policies have been in force, total demand has been stimulated by high government expenditure which has added to inflation instead of decreasing it. Recently, record levels of unemployment have added to the economic problems governments have had to face and made it more difficult for them to control inflation.

Income policies have helped to reduce inflation but they, in turn, have created problems. The most powerful groups of workers with the strongest bargaining power tend to receive the largest rises, leaving the weaker and poorer paid worse off than before. In the service industries, and others where productivity is difficult to measure, it is hard to decide what level of increase should be given and, generally, the question of comparability is raised. At the end of such a policy, when the period of restraint is seen to be over, although the need for it may still be very great, there is inevitably a surge of demands for large rises in wages and salaries to restore incomes to their previous real level.

The only permanent answer to the control of inflation is an increase in productivity—and consequently total production—that are easier said than achieved.

From the brief and simple account of one economic problem above it will be clear that many internal and external influences govern economic activity and performance. The government must try to influence and control these for the best interests of the country and its people, through measures which affect the supply of money in the economy, taxation and other controls. A full understanding of all these can only be gained by further reading, which should include press coverage of the current state of affairs. It will be realised that effective management of the economy is a very complex and difficult task.

The balance of payments

Trade with other countries involves changes of currency. When one buys something in Britain, one pays money for it since that is a simple and recognised means of exchange. Money is accepted by the buyer because of its purchasing power. When one buys a foreign product, the seller does not usually want pounds sterling in payment for it, since they do not have purchasing or exchange value in his country. He will, therefore, want to be paid in his own currency. In order to do this, the buyer will instruct his bank to purchase the value of Japanese yen or other foreign currency involved. This it will do through the Bank of England which holds a certain reserve of foreign currencies, thus enabling it to know the total stock of other countries' currencies held at any time. The bank will obtain the yen at the ruling rate of exchange between it and sterling, thereby reducing the Bank of England's holding of yen by £200, or whatever figure is involved, and increasing its stock of sterling by £200.

When goods are exported to other countries from Britain, the opposite obviously applies—the Bank of England's stock of foreign currency is increased and that of sterling decreased. All imports from and exports to other countries are transacted in this way, and at the end of the year the final totals of all foreign currency coming into the country and that going out of it, together with the total effect of transfers of capital, can be calculated. The difference between the two is the balance of payments. In short, it shows how well or badly Britain is paying her way in the world and whether she is adding to overseas assets or using them up. Generally, the two sides are fairly evenly balanced, but when more has been imported than sold abroad there is a balance of payments deficit, which means that Britain has to pay out more in foreign currency than she has received from abroad. This is clearly not a favourable position to be in. When there are indications that this is happening, the government takes action to correct it. If the government did not do this, it would have to use up its reserves of foreign currency to pay its debt, or borrow from another country or perhaps the International Monetary Fund in order to do so. Obviously, neither action is desirable and if taken will create a burden for the future.

Invisible exports, namely the selling of services such as insurance, banking, shipping and the income from visits of foreign tourists to Britain, make a very substantial contribution to the balance of payments since they bring a large and important amount of foreign currency to Britain each year.

The need for international trade arises because, clearly, every country cannot produce everything it wants or needs. Exchange of goods and services between countries means that each one has a greater variety. Then, as specialisation occurs, one country may be able to produce certain goods better or more cheaply than others. This leads to countries importing from abroad goods which they can produce at home, but it is more profitable for them to import particular items or services and export other goods instead, where their comparative advantage or gain is greater. This law of comparative costs applies more and more when deciding what to export and what to import, as technology becomes more advanced and more manufactured goods are exchanged between countries.

It can easily be seen that trade between countries is necessary and desirable for social and political as well as economic reasons. It is also realised that a persistent deficit in the balance of payments in any country is not desirable, and consequently tariffs and other controls are introduced to protect home industries, protect employment or reduce unemployment or help new industries to get on their feet by imposing an extra charge on imported goods, thereby making them less attractive and reducing demand for them. Although there may be many good economic and social benefits to the country imposing the controls and tariffs, the effect on the international scene is a reduction in total world trade—economic loss from which many countries suffer and very few gain. It is for this reason that, in recent years, there has been a general move to reduce tariffs and other restrictions to trade. The General Agreement on Tariffs and Trade (GATT) has been particularly keen and active to reduce tariffs. Although protective barriers to trade still exist, there is now more general movement towards free trade, in particular among a number of countries through the establishment of trading blocs such as the European Free Trade Area and the European Economic Community.

Trading blocs in Europe
Following the Second World War, developments were made to unite Europe. The Organisation for European Economic Co-operation was established in 1948, the Council of Europe in 1949 and the European Coal and Steel Community in 1952. The latter established a common market in coal and steel products and three of its member countries had previously formed a customs union. Several countries did not wish to be so deeply committed to unity in so many spheres and as a result seven countries, namely Austria, Denmark, Norway, Portugal, Sweden, Switzerland and the United Kingdom formed the European Free Trade Association, while the six continued to develop the European Community. The two groups developed alongside each other.

The aim of EFTA, as its name suggests, was simply to establish an association of countries with free trade among them for the benefit of them all. This was achieved for industrial goods but did not apply to most agricultural produce. Trade among the member countries increased, but Britain's trade with the EEC members increased by more than that with EFTA. This, and the advantages of belonging to a community with much deeper involvement than just free trade among members, together with the changing pattern of world trade, led Britain to join the EEC in 1973.

Membership of the European Economic Community
The EEC was created by the Treaty of Rome which was signed by Belgium, France, Germany (Federal Republic), Italy, Luxembourg and the Netherlands in 1957. Britain, Ireland and Denmark joined on 1 January 1973. Greece became a member in January 1981. Spain and

Portugal joined in January 1986. The Economic Community is one of three communities, each set up by a separate treaty, which make up the European Community. The Coal and Steel Community was the first to be established in 1952 and aimed to unite the coal and steel resources of the member countries, establish free trade between them for those raw materials and generally develop and assist the coal and steel industries as well as those employed in them. The third community is the European Atomic Energy Community (Euratom) established in 1957 to co-ordinate the development of the atomic and peaceful nuclear energy activities of member countries. As with coal and steel, a common market for all nuclear equipment and materials was established.

The aim of the European Economic Community is the balanced growth and development of the economies of member countries, through unity and integration. The introduction to the treaty included the following aims:

1. to establish foundations for growing unity among the people of Europe;
2. to improve working and living conditions;
3. to create free trade among member countries;
4. to assist overseas countries and the development of their economies.

To assist the attainment of these aims, internal tariffs and all other barriers to trade have been abolished, a common tariff has been imposed on goods entering the community from outside and a customs union has been established. Measures have been introduced to facilitate the free movement of labour, services and capital within the community. A common policy for agriculture was developed but remains subject to amendment in the light of the needs of member nations. Britain had particular problems in this sphere, having to make very large contributions to the Common Agricultural Policy (CAP) because of the system operating in the Community which is designed to help the small and relatively inefficient European farmer in countries that are more agriculturally based than Britain. Britain's farmers are extremely efficient and agriculture is a fairly small part of the total economy. As a result, Britain has to make very large contributions to the agricultural fund (larger than those of the more affluent members) even though she is one of the poorer members.

A review of the Community's budget has been promised. For the future development of the whole Community, it would seem necessary to re-allocate funds so that less is devoted to agriculture—which 1983 figures showed to be receiving more than 62 per cent of the total—and more is available for industrial, regional and social policies. There should also be some regard for and encouragement to new and important industries on which the future of each member country and that of the Community depends. This would seem to be in line with one of the Community's main objectives: to strengthen the economies of member states and encourage development by reducing regional differences through improving the economic levels of poorer countries.

Like other member states, Britain contributes to the Community budget a proportion (not exceeding 1 per cent) of the total revenue collected from value added tax (VAT), levies on agricultural imports and customs duties.

Many important policies and funds are already in existence. For example, the European Regional Development Fund provides financial help for industrial projects and those designed to improve the infrastructure in areas which are declining or are less developed. The European Social Fund provides finance for the training and re-training of young people, as well as for workers in declining industries. Britain has received substantial amounts of finance from both these funds, as well as grants and loans from the European Coal and Steel Community, the European Agricultural Guidance and Guarantee Fund and the European Investment Bank.

The European Monetary System was established in 1979, to encourage stability of exchange rates and lead to eventual monetary union. The pound sterling is included in the 'basket' of currencies which form the European Currency Unit, but Britain does not participate in the mechanism which determines rates of exchange. The European Currency Unit has become an important reserve currency.

Britain's membership of the European Community means that she must give up some freedom and sovereignty in exchange for economic, social and political gains. Community rules, for instance, have an important impact on firms, since they range from laws on the content of food products and the requirement to state their ingredients on the goods themselves, to legislation relating to mergers and monopoly power.

Probably the main argument in favour of Britain's membership of the Community is the political one that it made her part of a united Europe, which itself is important to the balance of world power. There are many economic advantages of membership too. Important among these are the wider markets which the Community offers to British industry and commerce and the opportunity to achieve economies of scale and comparative cost advantages. Most modern industry is so capital-intensive that large markets are essential to absorb the high levels of production needed to obtain low unit costs. In addition, technological advances in many industries require vast amounts of capital. Their potential is therefore greatest if projects are pursued jointly by various countries. In this way, capital is more easily raised and expertise is greater. The supersonic plane Concorde is a good example of a joint project. Joint ventures are clearly important, too, in areas such as nuclear and space research.

It is probably only through membership of a larger community that Britain can best hope to achieve greater economic growth with resulting higher living standards. Free trade should result in the best use of resources, encourage higher output and therefore a rise in gross national product, with a consequent increase in the standard of living. The higher growth rate among member countries provided an incentive for Britain to join the Community. However, economic growth is not so easily achieved. In order to take up the potential markets, output must be increased. That means a rise in productivity and possibly investment, and the resulting output must be what the market demands and at a competitive price. In short, improved economic performance is necessary in order to benefit from the potential which exists. An inevitable result of this is unemployment as demand falls for the products of declining industries. In order to progress, this labour must be retrained to meet the needs of newer and expanding industries. This means an economic cost to the country and the individuals concerned and requires labour to be adaptable and mobile, which poses social and personal problems. But these short-term costs should result in long-term benefits.

Since Britain joined the European Economic Community, there has been no significant improvement in the rate of her economic growth. The period of her membership, however, has been one of serious international economic problems, namely an energy crisis, inflation and depression. Britain's imports from members of the Community have remained greater than her exports to them. However, over 40 per cent of her total exports goes to member states.

Clearly, the world depression and rising levels of unemployment in several member countries make it more difficult for the Community to implement some of its policies; but perhaps they also emphasise the need to re-allocate resources, giving less prominence to agriculture, and considering how best to strengthen the economies of member states.

3 ────────────────────────────

NATIONAL INCOME

It is important for any country to be able to measure the value of the goods and services it produces during any particular period, in order to assess the amount and rate of change from one period to another, to indicate trends within the economy and to provide a means of comparing one country's economy and performance with that of another. The wealth of a country (or the total value of goods and services produced by it in any given period) is known as the *national income*. By its nature, this can never be an exact figure but it provides a useful guide to the wealth of a country at any given time. The value of goods and services produced by a country can be measured in three ways:

1. By totalling all the incomes received for producing them—income method;
2. By adding up all the money spent on purchasing them—expenditure method; *or*
3. By adding together the final value of output of each industry—output method.

National income is calculated each year for the United Kingdom, using all three methods so that there is a check on the relative accuracy of the figures produced. The figures are published annually in the National Income and Expenditure Blue Book.

When one uses the income method, incomes from all sources must be taken into account, in order to realise the value of the whole economy. This comprises income received from employment as wages and salaries, including that from self-employment; the income of companies, namely gross trading profits; the gross trading surpluses of nationalised industries and other organisations in public enterprise; and income from rent. The sum of income from all these sources produces the total value of goods and services produced in the country. This is known as *gross domestic product*. Other forms of income, namely rates of interest, dividends, social security benefits and private gifts are not included because they come from the forms of income described above—they are transfer payments—and have, therefore, already been calculated. The table on page 24 shows the calculation of national income for the United Kingdom for 1981 by the income method.

The same figure for gross domestic product is obtained by the expenditure method, where total expenditure by final buyers of all goods and services for consumption and investment is calculated. This comprises expenditure by individuals, government departments, nationalised industries, local authorities and private firms on day-to-day consumption, as well as their spending for investment. This can be defined simply as adding to wealth. It therefore includes fixed assets such as factories, plant, machinery, houses and other buildings, all of which constitute fixed investment or fixed capital formation. Investment also includes goods which are finished but not sold, work in the process of being finished, and stocks of raw materials. These forms of investment are known as capital formation in stocks. To the resulting total for expenditure on consumption and investment must be added the net difference between imports and exports. From this is subtracted the amount which has been paid in taxes on this expenditure and, conversely, the total for any subsidies which have been given is added. The result is the same as that obtained by the income method described above—gross domestic product—the total value of goods and services produced in the country.

The United Kingdom is a trading nation which is very involved in and dependent on trade with other countries. As a result, it has developed large and important investments overseas, which produce a significant income. Net property income from abroad, then, which is basically the total amount of interest, profit and dividend paid by firms and individuals abroad to people and institutions in the United Kingdom minus the total paid by this country to investors abroad, adds to the value of the country's wealth. The addition of this figure to the gross domestic product gives the *gross national product*. During the period for which calculations have been made, some capital will have been used in the form of machinery, buildings, plant and vehicles, in order to produce all the goods and services. So as to give a realistic account of the total production of wealth created, some deduction must be made for this depreciation or capital consumed. The result gives the final figure for *national income*.

FIG. A   *The National Income of the U.K. 1984*

Composition	£m	£m
Income from employment	180,342	
Income from self-employment[1]	26,885	
Gross trading profits of companies[1,2]	47,900	
Gross trading surplus of public corporations[1]	8,732	
Gross trading surplus of general government enterprises[1]	−250	
Rent[3]	18,937	
Imputed charge for consumption of non-trading capital	2,526	
Total domestic income	285,072	
less stock appreciation	(−5,163)	
Gross domestic product (income based)		279,909
Residual error		(−5,336)
Net property income from abroad		3,304
Gross national product (at factor cost)		277,877
less capital consumption		(−38,371)
National income (i.e., net national product)		239,506

[1] Before providing for depreciation and stock appreciation.
[2] Including financial institutions.
[3] Before providing for depreciation
Source: Central Statistical Office, 1985

The importance of national income

Everyone in a country is affected to some extent by the size of that nation's national income, since this gives the total value of goods and services or wealth produced in any given period and shows the total income available to the country as a whole. This, then, divided by the number of population, shows the national income per head, which puts wealth in perspective, since the larger the population, the less income there is available per person. Because standard of living is measured mainly by the amount of material possessions a person has, the standard of living of the people of any country depends first on the size of national income per head. Without a large national income per head, it is impossible to have a high standard of living for all. If a country has a high national income per head of population there can (but will not necessarily) be a high standard of living for everyone, since the actual standard of living of all the people obviously depends on how equally or otherwise the national income is distributed, what proportion of it is taken by the government in taxes and other ways, and how this is used. For instance, a country which has a high national income per head but whose government takes a large part of national income for investment and general development, will distribute a small proportion of income to the people who will, therefore, have a low current standard of living.

It will be appreciated that the standard of living in this sense is measured purely in material or economic terms. A high standard of living may not necessarily be a good thing. For instance, leisure may suffer in trying to produce more and more, and no calculation is made for any loss of health, freedom or enjoyment which may result.

Calculation of national income or gross national product provides a means of comparison between one country's economy and general standard of living and those of other countries.

Today there is much concern about economic growth. Calculation of national income each year enables us to measure how much of the economy has grown or contracted from one period to another, taking into account changes in prices and the value of money, i.e. changes in real terms that can be measured. Economic growth, then, describes an increase in gross domestic product or gross national product. This is important in order to provide increased resources and investment to continue to improve industrial development and modernisation, to improve and extend public services and to increase the standard of living. An indication of the rate of economic growth is obviously important to help planning and budgeting of the economy. The statistics also reveal in which sections of the economy growth has occurred, which is important for allocating resources, estimating the size of markets, etc. This information, together with that pertaining to the relationship between consumption, investment and total incomes, indicates to the government trends in the economy. Such information reveals where guidance, control and help are needed to establish desired movement and future trends.

Economic growth

There is much concern and discussion today about economic growth and whether it is a desirable goal. The reasons why countries aim for such growth have already been stated. It now remains to see how it can be achieved and the consequences. Economic growth was defined above as an increase in the total output of goods and services, taking into account inflation and changes in population. The means of achieving this depends first of all on the amount of spare capacity in the country in the form of land, labour, capital and enterprise. If there is plant, machinery, capital or labour unemployed or not fully employed, an increase in total output can obviously be achieved by utilising this spare capacity. If there are no unused resources, output can only be increased by raising productivity by increased investment or the application of improved technology to improve the output of existing resources. Similarly, new techniques to increase the production of labour and capital would also add to total production and consequently economic growth.

While the above points lead to economic growth, they are not easily achieved. Governments and society are largely ignorant of the reasons for different rates of economic growth, and many of the factors leading to it are difficult to measure as well as to achieve. Investment is one of these and, in order for it to be maintained at an adequate level, firms must be confident that their goods will sell in the future. Without this they obviously will not invest. Changes in government policies, usually arising from fear of inflation or balance of payments difficulties, resulting in stop–go policies, also hinder economic growth. In addition to these problems, we do not know what the optimum or desired level of economic activity is, either for an individual country or the world as a whole. Will world resources continue to expand to enable every country to develop its economy as it desires?

Economic growth has been the accepted aim of all advanced countries for many years, in order to improve living standards. These, however, as was mentioned when discussing national income, are measured purely in economic and material terms. It is now being realised that while economic growth increases certain standards, it reduces others. Although, in western countries, most people have more material possessions than ever before, they also suffer from increased pollution and congestion and many have to endure monotonous jobs and other penalties of progress and growth. It is important to realise that although higher growth is necessary to increase the standard of living, this higher standard does not necessarily follow from growth. However, the only way in which living standards, as we measure them, can rise is through economic growth, and we must decide whether to continue to aim for it. If we do decide that this is a worthwhile goal, all the factors of production will need to be more productive, more dynamic and certainly more mobile.

4

FORMS OF BUSINESS OWNERSHIP

Forms of business ownership in Britain fall into the two main categories already mentioned in the last chapter. Each of these can be further subdivided as shown below.

I PRIVATE ENTERPRISE
Sole Trader
Partnerships
Joint Stock Companies
Private
Public
Co-operatives

II PUBLIC ENTERPRISE
Direct Government Services
(Government Departments)
Public Corporations
Municipal Undertakings

For anything to work successfully, it must have a framework within which to operate.

One does not have to think hard to be aware of various forms and sizes of organisation, from the small one-man business, to a very large organisation owned by thousands of people, like ICI or British Leyland.

In order to understand the business world, on which we all depend, and in which many of us work, we must look at the various forms of ownership. We must examine how each one is financed and organised, how profit is allocated, and where the risk of loss lies. The next three chapters look at private enterprise and Chapters 7 to 10 inclusive concentrate on public enterprise.

I PRIVATE ENTERPRISE

The sole trader

This is the oldest and smallest form of ownership. It is as old as man himself. Today, with the strong tendency to large organisations and economies of large-scale production, we see fewer one-man owned businesses. Despite this, the sole trader is still the form of organisation most commonly found in the retail trade.

As the name implies, the sole trader business is one which is owned and controlled by one person. It is most prevalent in retailing and in trades where a personal service is provided and where a small capital outlay is required. Window cleaning, decorating and plumbing are good examples. Professional people too, like doctors and dentists, solicitors and accountants, often operate as sole traders.

In the field of retailing we can all readily call to mind at least one sole trader concern. It may be a general store, a newsagent and tobacconist, a mobile grocer's or greengrocer's shop, or a travelling hairdresser. In most cases, it comprises one single branch or shop.

Sole trader (or proprietor) concerns are run and managed by the owner, probably with the help of his family. Any profit which is made is his, but, conversely, he must also bear completely any losses which occur. He, therefore, has sole responsibility for all aspects of the business.

There are many advantages in this type of business, which accounts for the large numbers of sole traders still in existence. However, their numbers are declining, owing to the strong competition they are facing from supermarkets, other multiple organisations and chain stores.

A comparatively small amount of capital is needed to open a one-man business and, similarly, the overhead costs are usually fairly low, and can often be offset to a certain extent by using living accommodation on the premises. There are no legal formalities, so the business can be begun quickly and easily. The fact of being one's own boss is appealing to many people and has the advantage of enabling decisions and new ideas to be put into operation quickly. Members of the family are often available to help at busy times or on a part-time basis. This may also enable one to obtain extra business in the evenings or on Sundays when the larger stores are closed. The personal attention which can be given to customers is probably the greatest advantage the sole trader has over his large-scale competitors. Since profits are one's own, there is more incentive to work hard and introduce new ideas.

In contrast to these, we must not overlook the disadvantages which the sole trader faces. His lack of capital may prevent expansion. His small turnover and profit margin will prevent him from competing against the much lower prices which supermarkets and chain stores can offer as a result of their large-scale purchasing. A sole trader may lack the versatility required to manage efficiently all sides of the business. Because he has unlimited liability, in the event of bankruptcy he may have to sell his personal possessions in order to pay the debts of the firm. The sickness or death of the owner may mean that the business suffers because there is no one available to manage it adequately.

To summarise, because the sole trader owns his business completely, he provides all its capital, has the sole responsibility for running and managing it and therefore reaps all the profit or, conversely, if it goes bankrupt, must bear the total loss.

Partnerships

As the sole trader's business prospers he may decide to expand his existing premises or open another branch. To do this he will need extra capital. He may also require help in organising the business. One way of achieving both of these is to form a partnership, of which there are two types.

1. *Ordinary partnership*

Number of members	Two to twenty. (Can be extended for certain professions)
Liability	Unlimited for all members.
Powers	Each partner can take an active part in running the business.
Profit	Shared among the partners.
Legal requirements	None.
Publishing of Annual Accounts	Not compulsory.

Any number of people from two to twenty can join together to form a partnership. The Partnership Act of 1890 defined this form of organisation as 'The relation which subsists between persons carrying on a business in common with a view to profit.' It is easy to begin, since there are no legal requirements, and as a form of organisation it offers many advantages. In short, it makes extra capital, help with management, and often specialist skills available to a business, together with the sharing of risk.

Each partner can take an active part in the business and bind it to a certain course of action. Profits are usually shared according to the amount of capital each partner has subscribed, and this fact is stated in the partnership agreement. If no such agreement has been drawn up, or if the conditions in it are not clear, then the provisions of the Partnership Act 1890 apply. This states that the profits must be shared equally.

In addition to bringing more capital into a business, a partner will introduce new blood in the form of new ideas and often specialist skills. Two partners in a catering concern, for instance, may successfully run the business by letting one take responsibility for the administration and office side of the work while the other specialises in the actual catering.

The advantage of maintaining personal contact with customers and suppliers exists in the partnership as much as in the one-man business. The fact of being able to discuss future plans and business problems with others who have a vested interest in the concern is an obvious point in favour of the partnership, as is the fact that if one partner is away on holiday or absent because of illness there is someone else to carry on the business efficiently. In the event of the death or retirement of one of the partners, the continuity of the business is assured.

When a partnership is formed it is wise to draw up a partnership agreement setting out the terms and conditions of the firm to cover any difficulties or disagreements which may occur in the future. The actual contents of such an agreement or deed will obviously vary from one firm to another but it will usually contain information as to the name of the firm, and its partners, together with their addresses, the nature of the business, the amount of capital to be subscribed by each partner, the method and proportions of sharing profits and losses, the amount of control each partner should have, the amount of salary each partner may have and whether interest should be payable on advances which partners make to the firm in addition to their initial subscribed capital, and conditions of the dissolution of the partnership. In the absence of a partnership agreement, or where the provisions of such a document are silent or ambiguous, the provisions of the Partnership Act of 1890 apply. This provides for each partner to have a share in the running and management of the firm, for profits and losses to be shared equally among the members, for interest of five per cent to be paid on advances made in addition to the initial agreed capital, and states that no salaries shall be paid.

The conditions and comments stated above apply to ordinary or active partners, but it is also possible to contribute capital and receive a share of the profits without taking any share in the running of the business. A person entering a partnership on this basis is known as a dormant, sleeping or silent partner.

From what has been said about the general partnership, it is easy to see why it is such a popular form of organisation for professional people, for others providing a service, and for some retailing concerns. It should also be noted that, because of the principle of unlimited liability which all the members of an ordinary or general partnership must accept, the public is protected from any losses which the firm may suffer, since these must be borne by the partners.

From the point of view of the partners, the principle of unlimited liability is a disadvantage, for it means that in the event of the failure of the business each partner, whether active or sleeping, can be held responsible for all the debts of the firm, even to the extent of selling his own personal possessions in order to pay them. Clearly, since each partner can bind the firm to a certain course of action, one partner could find himself responsible for all the debts of the firm because of the mistakes of the other partners. This is a very great risk which prevents some people from entering partnerships. Similarly, the fact that the partnership is not a legal entity means that each partner has complete involvement legally for all the actions of the firm. Another disadvantage is that it is often difficult to obtain extra capital beyond that provided by the partners, or to replace that of a partner who leaves. Friction or disagreements between partners can hinder progress and ultimately, in some cases, break up the partnership.

2. *Limited partnership*

Number of members	Two to twenty. (Can be extended for certain professions).
Liability	Limited but *at least* one member must have unlimited liability.

Powers	The ordinary partner(s) has responsibility for management and control of the business. Limited partners have no say in the control of the business.
Legal requirements	Agreement must be registered with the Registrar of Companies.
Publishing of Annual Accounts	Not compulsory.

The limited partnership was introduced by the Limited Partnership Act of 1907. This recognised the hazardous nature of the ordinary partnership and the act was passed to make it easier to raise extra capital, and to enable an existing partner to leave the firm without withdrawing his capital and, at the same time, limiting his liability to the amount of that capital.

The limited partnership is similar to the ordinary or general partnership, except that as long as there is at least one ordinary partner who has unlimited liability and is responsible for the management and running of the firm, the remaining members can be limited partners, i.e. their liability or risk is limited to the amount of capital they subscribe to the business. In the event of the failure of the firm, the limited partners lose the capital they have contributed, but any remaining debts must be paid by the ordinary partner(s). Because their risk of loss is limited, the limited partners cannot take an active part in the running of the firm. They merely invest capital in the business and are paid interest on it. Provided they have the consent of the general partners they can transfer their share of the firm at any time. In simple terms, the limited partners are really dumb financiers to the business.

This type of partnership is suitable for a business which requires extra capital without intervention. A retailer who requires additional capital to expand his business but wishes to retain sole control over it may form a limited partnership.

It is not a very popular form of organisation, since the private company affords all the advantages which the limited partnership offers together with the additional ones of limited liability for all members and the ability to raise more capital.

Joint-stock companies

A joint-stock company is one which is owned collectively by a number of people. The first Companies Act was passed in 1844, and since that time the government has exercised constant surveillance by frequent revisions and additions to the laws governing this type of commercial organisation. As an example, there was a major new Companies Act in 1967, but there have been further acts in 1976, 1980 and 1981. Without any doubt, more can be expected and the student must be alert to such changes.

There are two types of joint-stock or limited company, namely the private company and the public company.

1. *Private limited company*

Number of members	Minimum two. No upper limit.
Liability	Limited for all members.
Power and control	Control by Board of Directors who are elected by the shareholders. Transfer of shares is restricted.
Profit	Divided among shareholders according to type and amount of shares held.
Legal requirements	Articles and Memorandum of Association must be registered with the Registrar of Joint Stock Companies and a Certificate of Incorporation obtained before trading can begin.
Publishing of Annual Accounts	Compulsory.
Capital	Contributed by the shareholders.

The private company is a very popular form of organisation. In fact, it accounts for about 97 per cent of all the companies in Britain. Its greatest advantage is that all its members have limited liability. This accounts for the word 'limited' which must appear in the name of every private and public limited company. Its purpose is to inform all those dealing with the company that its members have limited liability and consequently, in the event of the failure of the business, can only lose the amount of money they have invested in it. Any remaining debts may not be paid, but die with the company. Once a company is formed it becomes a legal entity which means that in the eyes of the law it is an individual entirely separate from its shareholders so they cannot be held responsible for its debts.

The private company, having no upper limit to the number of its members, can raise more capital than the partnership. As its name suggests, however, the private company may not appeal to the public for money but must obtain shareholders by personal contact. Other advantages of this form of organisation are that it has automatic continuity on the retirement or death of a shareholder, whereas in a partnership the firm has to be re-formed. While retaining all the above advantages, it is also possible for the private company to be small enough to preserve personal contact between the directors, staff, suppliers and customers and not suffer from the disadvantages of bureaucracy which often exist in larger organisations.

The private limited company is a very popular form of organisation in retailing and the building industry. For a small retailer who wishes to expand his business but keep control within his family, the private company is ideal.

The disadvantage of the private company is that it cannot appeal to the public for capital. However, the Companies Act 1980 made it easier for private companies to expand, by removing the previous limit of fifty members. The Act also removed the earlier restrictions on transfer of shares and, as a result, made investment in a private company more attractive to potential shareholders. However, a company which wishes to ensure that shares are sold to existing shareholders and persons of whom the directors approve, or wishes to impose other restrictions on the transfer of shares, may do so by stating the requirements in the Articles of Association.

2. *Public limited company*

Number of members	Minimum two—no upper limit.
Liability	Limited for all members.
Power and control	Control by Board of Directors who are elected by the shareholders. Shares freely transferable.
Profit	Divided among shareholders according to number and type of shares held.
Legal requirements	Memorandum and Articles of Association must be submitted to the Registrar of Joint Stock Companies and a Trading Certificate obtained before it can commence trading.

	Must have 'Public Limited Company' at the end of its name, or initials PLC.
Annual Accounts	Publishing compulsory.
Capital	May appeal to the public for initial and additional capital.
	Must have an allotted share capital of not less than £50,000 (nominal value).

The public limited company, though not the most numerous, is the most important form of company organisation in Britain. Today, as industrial and other concerns are becoming larger, its importance is increasing, since it is the only form of organisation which provides the means of raising the large amounts of capital needed to finance them.

The reasons for the importance of this form of company organisation are obvious. The absence of an upper limit on the number of members makes it easy to raise the large sums of capital required initially and also any additional capital needed. Limited liability for all members encourages members of the public to invest. An important advantage which the public company has over all other forms of organisation in private enterprise is the easy and quick exchange of shares possible through the Stock Exchange. Because people know that they can sell their shares at any time, they are more willing to buy them. The different types of share offered by most large companies means that they appeal to various types of investors. The large amounts of capital which public limited companies can obtain make it possible for them to take advantage of large-scale economies and production and carry out research and development which, in turn, benefit the consumer in the form of new, better and cheaper products.

Continuity is another advantage of the public company, for it will continue to exist after directors have left. The separation of ownership and control means that specialists in the field of management can be employed while the directors continue to specialise at their level. Lastly, but by no means least in importance, there is the fact that the investing public is protected as far as possible against bad management in public companies by the close scrutiny exercised by the Registrar of Joint Stock Companies (a government office) and the Stock Exchange before a public company can be formed, and at the end of each year when its accounts are examined by the Registrar. These controls inspire the public's confidence in the public company and make it more willing to invest money in the hope that the value of the shares will rise and/or will pay good dividends.

While the advantages of the public limited company easily outweigh the disadvantages, the latter must be considered.

The first drawback is the costly and lengthy process of floating or setting up the company. Secondly, although in theory the shareholders have control over the business, in practice they have little say in the running of it. The Board of Directors makes the decisions regarding the policy of the firm and the management must clearly make the day-to-day decisions. Size automatically brings disadvantages in the form of lack of personal contact—the workers and the customers of a firm rarely see the directors and are not even aware of the names of the shareholders because of their large numbers, together with the fact that shareholders are constantly changing. Size also frequently causes delay in decision-making. Bureaucracy, too—red tape and official-dom—is often present in the large concern and is criticised for restricting individual initiative and progress. Size may also give rise to disagreement between workers and management, shareholders and management or even among shareholders themselves. The requirement of the Companies Act 1980 for a firm to state 'Public Limited Company' in its name, makes its status clear to everyone.

Holding and subsidiary companies

A company owning fifty per cent or more of the voting shares in another firm has a controlling interest in it and is therefore referred to as a controlling, parent or sometimes a holding company. However, a holding company is usually one which holds shares in subsidiaries and co-ordinates them financially but does not actually trade itself. Through this means, a holding company can gain control of subsidiary companies with a minimum financial outlay and obtain the advantages of large-scale production, while the subsidiaries retain their individuality and a measure of control.

A subsidiary can purchase shares in another firm and become a parent company in its own right, while still remaining a subsidiary itself.

Where a group of companies under common control hold a large share of a market they are commonly referred to as a combine.

The Co-operative Movement

This is a unique and democratic form of organisation. It was the first consumer-orientated shopping movement.

A business run on a co-operative basis is one which is owned by its customers. The co-operative movement in Britain has been successful in distribution, i.e. in wholesaling and retailing.

The first successful retail society was formed in Rochdale in 1844 when twenty-eight weavers grouped together to form the Rochdale Pioneers. They each contributed £1 and the resulting total of £28 was used to open a general store. The profits from this were then shared among the customers who had contributed to them, according to the value of the purchases they had made. This is still the distinguishing feature of co-operatives—their customers are their owners.

Today, following the many mergers which have taken place during the last few years, there are 165 retail co-operative societies in the United Kingdom and more than thirteen million members. Every society operates on the same basis but each one is completely independent from the rest. It must therefore provide its own capital and control and manage its own affairs.

Any one over the age of sixteen may become a member of a retail co-operative society by buying a £1 share. He then receives a share of its profits in the form of dividend on his purchases. When the dividend is declared the customer can withdraw his amount in cash or leave it in the society where it becomes share capital and receives interest, usually at 5 per cent per annum. The maximum investment any member can have is £10,000. This money is available to the society for development, expansion, investment and current needs.

Since the customers or members of a society are its owners, they must control the business as well as receive its profits. To this end, they are entitled to attend quarterly meetings where, contrary to other forms of business organisation, each member has one vote regardless of the amount of share capital he possesses. He is able to vote on matters of policy and for the election of members for the Committee of Management which is responsible for running the society. The work of this committee or board can be compared to that of the board of directors of a company.

Retail co-operative societies are active in almost every form of retailing, from grocery to funeral directing, and own all forms of retail outlets from the department store and supermarket to the mobile shop. One only has to think of a large co-operative society to realise the wide range of activities it is involved in. The system of self-service in the grocery trade in Britain was introduced by a co-operative society and co-operative societies have also been pioneers in other fields.

Present trends

While membership of co-operative societies continued to increase, the amount of purchases per member fell steadily for a time. Societies suffered severe competition from the large multiple organisations, and their share of the total retail trade consequently dropped, but picked up during the 1970s. In recent years the societies have made a conscious effort to modernise their whole operation to fit modern selling patterns and consumer preferences. Their original image as a predominantly working-class organisation was replaced by an appeal to a wider group of customers. The concept of membership was retained, although the dividend was displaced in most stores by trading stamps, exchangeable for goods or cash. The former emphasis on 'own brands' gave way to a less restricted policy, and Co-op shops stock a high proportion of well-known brands at competitive prices. They have also adopted sales promotion methods such as cut-price offers and other marketing attractions.

Problems also had to be faced in management, where it was necessary to attract top quality personnel. The traditional democratic pattern of the Co-op had been criticised for its amateur character and loss of efficiency, partly because of the system of allowing shareholders to elect management committees. These committees now appoint professional managers, but there is still the need to attract dynamic management in order to facilitate the structural changes necessary for future progress and survival.

The amalgamation of many of the smaller societies with others has made more viable businesses which can benefit from economies of larger scale operating and thereby compete more easily with other retail outlets. Advertising, particularly on television, and other changes such as the brightening up of delivery vans and the offer of a wider variety of goods in the shops are helping to improve the image of the co-operatives and bring them into the public eye. Finally, one of the most important recent changes has been to make the Co-operative Wholesale Society almost a guide or father figure for the retail societies. This has meant the promotion of a co-ordinated and integrated policy for the whole country. In recent years, several regional societies have been formed and proved very successful. Their broader base has enabled them to co-ordinate and consolidate finance, management and effort, as well as expand markets and enter new trades. The result has been increased trade. This trend has been extended further by the merging of retail societies into twenty-six regional groups based on the largest and strongest societies. These and other plans to modernise the Co-op's image can only bring improved results. They are necessary if the movement is to survive and prosper in the very competitive and rapidly changing field of distribution.

Summarised Organisation of a Co-operative Society

Owners .... Customers = members
Capital provided by .... Customers = members
Profits distributed to .... Customers = members
Control exercised by .... Customers = members
(Compare with summary for the CWS)

The Co-operative Wholesale Society
The CWS operates on the same basis as the retail societies which own and control it. They provide its capital by maintaining a membership subscription based on the size of their own membership (a minimum of £5 for every two members in each retail society) and receive its profits according to the amount of purchases they have made from it. The Wholesale Society is run and managed by a Board of Directors elected by the retail societies.

As its name suggests, the CWS has warehouses situated in various parts of the country from which it supplies the retail societies with goods. It is also involved in manufacturing and owns over 100 under-takings which manufacture groceries and provisions. It operates bacon factories in Denmark and owns tea-growing estates in India and Sri Lanka. The Co-operative Bank and Insurance Society are also included in the Wholesale Society's activities.

Summarised Organisation of the Co-operative Wholesale Society

Owners	Retail Societies = members and
	customers
Capital provided by	Retail Societies
Profits distributed to	Retail Societies
Control exercised by	Retail Societies

5

SOURCES OF CAPITAL

Share capital

Every business needs capital to begin and carry on trading. In the case of the sole trader concern, the owner must provide all this himself. Similarly, in the partnership the partners, who are the sole owners and managers of the firm, supply its capital. Short-term finance is often borrowed.

Public companies raise long-term capital from members of the public who become shareholders. They are able to choose from different types of share. These are issued to appeal to different types of people according to the amount of risk they wish to take.

There are two broad classes of share, namely preference and ordinary. (The latter are known as equities.) They vary basically in the rights and responsibilities they give to their holders. Companies must initially issue their capital in the form of shares. Each share is a unit of capital and therefore forms part of the company. For example, money one subscribes for shares may be used to purchase part of a wall or be put towards the cost of furniture or machinery. Once it has been raised, therefore, the company has this money permanently. Through the services of the Stock Exchange, investors may change, but the total share capital of any company remains the same unless a further issue is made. The full amount of authorised capital is not always raised initially; the balance can then be issued at any time.

Having decided the nominal or par value of the shares, which is the price at which they are issued, a company need not ask shareholders for the total amount but can leave a balance to be called on if it is needed in the future. If the shares change hands in the meantime, the new owner is liable to pay the balance when it is called for. Prospective shareholders should discover whether or not shares are fully paid up before purchasing them.

Preference shares

These shares carry the least risk. As their name suggests, their holders are given preference in that they are the first to be paid a dividend and have first claim on the company's assets in the event of its failure. Preference shares normally carry a fixed dividend, e.g. 5 per cent preference shares. This is sure to be paid, even on occasions when the holders of ordinary shares receive no dividend. The only occasion when they are not paid is, of course, when the company makes no profit or a loss.

There are several types of preference share, namely:

Cumulative preference shares.   If there have been insufficient profits to pay a dividend for any period, the first year a profit is made the holders of cumulative preference shares will receive the appropriate dividend for that year, together with the cumulative amount for the years when no dividend was paid. They are entitled to this before any other class of shareholder is paid.

Participating preference shares.   The holders of these shares participate in the prosperity of the firm, since in addition to a fixed dividend they receive an agreed share of the remaining profits.

Redeemable preference shares.   These shares give the company the right to pay back to shareholders the money they have invested, and the shareholders the right to sell their shares back to the company. This process is governed by very strict conditions which are specified in the Companies Act.

People who want a fairly safe investment, and are content with a sure but comparatively small dividend, will buy preference shares.

Ordinary shares

Ordinary shares or equities form the largest part of the share capital of most firms. They carry the greatest risk, since their holders receive dividend from what is left of the profits after all the other classes of shareholder have been paid. Similarly, they have the last claim on the assets of the company in the event of failure of the business.

The rate of dividend varies from year to year according to the profit the firm has made. The holder of ordinary shares, therefore, may get a high dividend if the profit is good, or none at all if there is too little or no profit. When times are good the ordinary shareholder will usually obtain a good dividend, but when they are difficult and the company's profits are low he may receive nothing.

People who buy ordinary shares do so either with the intention of selling them at a later date, when they hope the price will have risen, thereby making a profit, or because of the dividend they hope to obtain from them each year. It should be remembered here that dividend is paid on the nominal or par value of shares, which may be very different from the market price a shareholder has paid for them. A dividend of 20 per cent on a 25p (nominal value) share is 5p, but if the share costs £2 to buy, this represents a yield of only 2½ per cent on what was paid for it. There is a strong argument in favour of no par value shares where the dividend would be declared as a fixed sum per share, e.g. 5p per share. As yet none of these has been issued in Britain.

Ordinary shares give their holders the right to vote at shareholders' meetings. Voting rights are determined by the company, but are usually one vote for each share held. Some companies issue non-voting shares which are described as 'A' or 'B' shares. There is no standard meaning implied by these letters, so wherever they are used the intending investor should carefully look into their meaning and the consequent rights and responsibilities.

A shareholder who is entitled to attend a meeting has the right to appoint a proxy to attend and vote in his place. Since companies are legal entities in the eyes of the law, they can hold shares in other companies. Where this does arise, directors can appoint a representative to vote and act on the company's behalf.

Debentures

Debenture holders are creditors of a company, not members of it, and therefore have no voting rights. They are entitled to a fixed rate of interest which must be paid whether or not the company makes a profit. Debentures are loans made to a company on security, for a fixed period of time, say, thirty years, or repayable at notice, in which case a stated period of notice specified in the debenture must be given by the company in order to redeem them. Some debentures are irredeemable, that is, they are only repaid in the event of liquidation.

A register of debenture holders is retained by the company and kept up-to-date when changes in ownership occur through buying and selling on the Stock Exchange.

Raising extra capital

A firm requiring extra capital permanently will raise it through an issue of shares. If there are any partly paid up shares, it will first consider calling on the capital outstanding.

In most cases, it is necessary to make a further issue of shares. If the authorised capital has not been fully issued, it can issue the balance. If there is none, arrangements will have to be made for a new issue. This process will be the same as that for floating a new company as explained in Chapter 4 and will usually be carried out by an issuing house.

If the capital is not required permanently the company will have to consider all the methods available for raising money. It will, of course, first investigate the possibility of raising it within the firm. If this is not possible, the method chosen will depend upon the amount of money required, the length of time for which it is required and the reason for its being needed.

In most cases, money required for a short period of time will be obtained by an overdraft from a bank. This may be necessary to bridge the gap between expenditure which must be paid on one date and income being received later, or for some seasonal demand like increase in stock. Sometimes even this form of borrowing can be avoided by bringing in money owing to the firm or extending credit.

Money needed for more than a short-term period can be raised in several ways. Property can be sold. The freehold of land and buildings can be sold, or a loan raised on mortgage of land and buildings.

Banks will, of course, lend money on security for short, medium and long-term periods. The ease with which loans can be obtained depends on the economic state of the country and government restrictions on credit at any given time. If none of these means is adequate to satisfy a firm's needs, or if it is too small to raise capital through the stock market, it can approach Finance for Industry Limited. This was established in 1973 as a holding company to link together the Industrial and Commercial Finance Corporation and the Finance Corporation for Industry, both of which had been established in 1945. The shares in Finance for Industry Limited are held by the clearing banks and the Bank of England. The main objective of this institution is to provide medium- and long-term finance at fixed rates of interest for small- and medium-sized firms. It will often lend for longer periods than the banks.

Leasing is becoming increasingly popular as a means of obtaining plant or equipment without drawing on capital. A machine, vehicle or other item may be obtained on lease by paying an agreed rental at regular intervals, so that firms are paying out of income while using the equipment. At the end of the agreement, the asset is returned to the leasing company. This method of payment has the added attraction of tax relief.

6

THE STOCK EXCHANGE

Function

This is one of the most important institutions in Britain. Everyone depends on its existence. It is the pinnacle around which the financial structure of the country revolves. In the London Stock Exchange, which is the largest in the world, some 7,200 securities are dealt with. These include the stocks and shares of public companies, government stock, local authority issues and foreign and Commonwealth stocks.

The function of the Stock Exchange, although vitally important, is very simple. It provides a market place where buyers and sellers can meet. It differs from most other markets in three ways. First, it deals with intangible commodities, namely stocks and shares. Secondly, it is a free market—the prices of stocks and shares are determined solely by the supply of and demand for them. Lastly, it deals with existing securities—stocks and shares which have already been issued but are changing hands. In doing this, the Stock Exchange equates two needs. Companies require large amounts of money to commence and continue trading. This is required in cash, and must be permanent, since it is absorbed in buildings and equipment. Members of the public, on the other hand, have money which they wish to invest provided that they can withdraw it if they wish or if some other need arises. While the Stock Exchange plays no direct part in the issue of new securities, indirectly it is the main reason for the public's willingness to buy stocks and shares.

Origin

Like many other important British institutions, the Stock Exchange was born out of need. During the seventeenth century, trade with other countries was expanding and extra capital was required. Merchants realised that members of the public were willing to invest money in their trading ventures in return for a dividend. Investors who wanted their money back for some reason had to find someone else willing to buy their shares from them. This was often a long and difficult process. The price obtained for the shares would depend on the number for sale at any one time and the number of people wishing to buy them. This gave rise to agents, or brokers, who specialised in buying and selling shares. They were viewed with suspicion at first, because of the variations in the prices of securities.

These early stockbrokers first met at the Royal Exchange, but later moved to coffee houses in the City area of London. Here the waiters used to take messages and run errands for them. As a result, the attendants at the London Stock Exchange are still called waiters.

The first Stock Exchange was opened in 1773, on the corner of Threadneedle Street. A second building was erected on the same site in 1853. This was rebuilt to form the present building which was completed in 1972. Business continued as usual during the rebuilding on a restricted area of the floor. The Stock Exchange has trading floors in Birmingham, Dublin, Glasgow, Liverpool and Manchester.

Members

Unlike most other markets the London Stock Exchange only allows members and their authorised clerks on the floor of the exchange. There are two types of member—brokers and jobbers.

Brokers

People wishing to buy or sell stocks or shares have to contact a broker to do this for them. He is an agent who will buy or sell stocks and shares in any company, or government securities on behalf of his clients. He will give advice free of charge and buy or sell shares at his clients' request in return for commission. Like most professional people, stockbrokers are not allowed to advertise for business. A list of brokers can be obtained from the London Stock Exchange or from any of the local exchanges.

Jobbers

The work of jobbers is even more specialised than that of the brokers, since they deal in only one particular market of securities, e.g. mines, stores or motors. They work on the floor of the exchange and actually have possession of the securities which they are willing to buy or sell. They do not deal directly with the public, but only with brokers.

The jobber is a highly-skilled man whose income is derived from the difference between the price at which he buys securities and that at which he sells them. This difference in prices is known as the 'jobber's turn'. He decides prices purely according to the supply of and demand for each particular security at any one time. Since this can fluctuate almost from minute to minute, and the jobber stands to lose by making a wrong decision, this task is a highly skilled one. Because of it prices are always representative of supply and demand. The system of jobbers is unique to the London Stock Exchange.

While the main function of the Stock Exchange to provide a market in securities has not changed, its organisation and methods of operation have been involved in an almost continuous but gradual revolution to keep up to date with changes in the needs and responses of investors. Not least among the changes has been the effect of the 1967 Companies Act, which removed the restriction on brokers' and jobbers' firms to have a maximum of twenty partners. Together, these and other changes have brought about an increase in the size of firms and a programme of rationalisation.

Procedure for buying or selling securities

A person wishing to buy or sell shares, debentures or government stock, which is known as gilt-edged security, must contact a broker who then goes to the Stock Exchange where he meets the jobbers dealing in the appropriate market and circulates among them to obtain the best price. The floor of the exchange is divided into sections, each representing a particular market.

When the broker approaches each jobber, he merely states the name of the firm in whose shares his client is interested and the class of security. The jobber, not knowing whether he wants to buy or sell, quotes two prices, say £2.55 and £2.56. The lower is the price at which he will buy and the higher that at which he will sell, the difference between the two being the jobber's turn. Having obtained several quotations, the broker will return to the jobber offering the best bargain and clinch the deal. The broker and jobber each make a note of the transaction in their notebooks but no documents are exchanged at this stage, hence the motto of the Stock Exchange: 'Dictum meum pactum'—my word is my bond.

After the Stock Exchange has closed at 3.00 p.m. each day, brokers and jobbers return to their offices to deal with the paperwork relating to each transaction.

On the day that the broker has bought or sold securities for his client, he notifies him of this by sending him a contract note, which gives details of the transaction including the amount of broker's commission. The broker's next task is to inform the company concerned of the change of ownership so that its Register of Shareholders can be corrected accordingly. The seller of shares must return his share certificate when he sells his shares, thereby giving up the legal proof of his ownership. A new share certificate is issued to the buyer by the company, soon after the transaction has been completed.

Payment

The year is divided into twenty-four 'accounts' periods which are usually of two weeks' duration and end on a Friday. These dates are always clearly shown in the financial pages of the daily newspapers. Anyone who buys shares during an account does not have to pay for them until 'Account (or Settlement) Day' which occurs on the second Tuesday after the end of an account.

Eight days before Settlement Day, i.e. the Monday immediately after an account is Contango Day (or continuation day) on which any arrangements to delay settlement must be made. Such delayed payments incur charges called 'contango'.

If the seller cannot deliver the shares on time he must pay a charge known as 'backwardation', to the buyer.

Payment for and delivery of gilt-edged securities cannot be postponed.

Speculation

During an account period the price of a security may change considerably. Someone who buys shares at the beginning of the account and sells them at a higher price before Contango Day will not pay out any money, but merely receive the difference between his buying and selling price. Conversely, if the price falls and he sells, he will have to pay the difference in price.

A speculator buys and sells shares quickly to make a profit. There are two main types of speculator. A 'bull' buys shares in the hope that the price will rise so that he can sell them and make a profit. A 'bear' sells shares he does not hold with the intention of buying them at a lower price before Contango Day when he has to deliver them. Consequently the term a 'bull market' is used to describe one of rising prices and financial confidence. The opposite is a 'bear market' where economic trends are uncertain and prices are falling or expected to fall.

The speculator who buys new issues of shares with the intention of selling them as soon as possible to make a profit, is called a 'stag'.

In practice, of course, speculators use all three methods.

Speculators provide a service because they help to steady the market. By buying when prices are low they help to increase them and, conversely, by selling when prices are high, they help to bring them down. Speculation only accounts for something in the region of 3 per cent of total investment.

The average shareholder buys shares mainly for one of two reasons. Either he buys at a certain price with the intention of selling the shares at some future date when the prices rise by a sufficient amount, and thereby making a profit, or he buys for the return which the shares will provide in the form of dividend.

The Stock Exchange Council

The London Stock Exchange is governed by an elected council of forty-seven plus five lay members. The council analyses applications by firms who wish their shares to be quoted on the exchange. Very stringent requirements have to be met before a quotation is given.

In addition to managing the Stock Exchange and ensuring the protection of the public against fraudulent or doubtful companies, the Stock Exchange Council has also done much to inform the public about the work of the Stock Exchange and remove the view that it exists only for the wealthy. The visitors' gallery is open to the public and people may watch brokers and jobbers at work, while listening to an explanatory commentary. The Council provides lecturers, has made films which are available free of charge, and published many useful booklets and leaflets on the work of the exchange.

There are still relatively few direct investors in Britain. However, two out of every three adults in Britain are indirect investors on the Stock Exchange, since banks, insurance companies, pension funds, trade unions and other similar bodies invest part of their funds in stocks and shares, thereby enabling them to pay to their members a higher rate of interest or dividend than they would otherwise be able to give. Direct investors number only about 4,000,000 people.

The Wider Share Ownership Council formed for the specific purpose of familiarising people with the functions and workings of the Stock Exchange, has done much to remove barriers of ignorance and fear.

Share prices

The market price of any shares at any time is determined by the supply of and demand for them. The Stock Exchange merely reflects the moods and actions of investors in the prices of stocks and shares. As with other markets, price is the means of equating demand with supply. Because the supply of any shares is fixed at any given time, a heavy demand will force prices up and a small or decreasing demand will push them down, so that the market price of shares reflects the public's opinion of the state of the particular company at any given time.

Unlisted Securities Market

An important addition to the traditional services of the Stock Exchange was made when the Unlisted Securities Market was introduced in 1980. This enabled firms to obtain a public quotation for their shares more easily and cheaply than with a full Stock Exchange listing. Only 10 per cent of shares need be offered to the public, a company need only have been trading for a minimum of three years, there is no initial listing fee and the annual fee is substantially less than the amount required for a full listing. In addition, companies can save a substantial amount of money by not having to publicise their full prospectus in newspapers. The USM has made it possible for many companies, particularly medium and smaller ones, to appeal to the public for capital. The market is gaining increasing support from the institutions and public generally, since the Stock Exchange investigations and support—although much less than in the case of full listings—are sufficient to provide the investor with confidence.

Note

Major changes in the method of operation of the Stock Exchange will take place with the so-called 'Big Bang' in October 1986. These will include the phasing out of standard commission so that each member will be free to charge what he wishes. The distinction between broker and jobber will disappear. There will simply be dealers in securities. Many restrictions will go and there will be increased competition between firms dealing in stocks and shares. The scope of each firm will be broadened. Already many banks have joined with dealers of stocks and shares, and foreign banks as well as others involved in the capital and money markets are buying into dealer firms.

7

THE GOVERNMENT IN THE COMMERCIAL WORLD

II PUBLIC ENTERPRISE

The government of any country is really its trustee or guardian. It is responsible for its general and financial management, its protection and the general welfare of its people. As time goes by these functions become more complex and governments take more responsibility for the performance of the economy.

In recent years, the main aim of successive British governments has been to achieve full employment and a faster rate of economic growth through an increase in the total output per head to provide a faster rise in living standards. Combined with these, they have sought the achievement and maintenance of a greater degree of price stability and a stronger balance of payments position. Greater price stability is an important factor in making home-produced goods competitive with imports. This in turn is necessary to obtain and maintain a strong balance of payments, which is essential to the achievement of full employment and a maintained faster rate of growth.

These expansionist policies have resulted in rapid increases in demand which have not been accompanied by sufficient increases in supply. Increased prices have been the result and a contributory cause of the consequent balance of payments deficit. In attempts to correct this inflationary spiral, governments have pursued policies to reduce the increase in demand. These have led to an improvement in the balance of payments, but also to a slowing down in the growth of output and rises in the level of unemployment. Expansionist policies have then followed which have again caused balance of payments deficits. While this vicious circle has shown that governments have failed to achieve all four objectives at the same time, they have had a large measure of success in other spheres and have ensured the maintenance of Great Britain as a world power.

The government at any time must guide and control the economy to make ends meet and provide for the future. The policies and strategy it employs to achieve this will depend upon its political ideals and international and national events. A country, like a firm or a person, is not isolated. It exists in a world with other nations and powers. It trades with them and is affected by their actions and by events which affect them. Situations can occur which are completely beyond the foresight and control of the government but which affect the country and the implementation of political policies. Britain, because of her dependence on foreign trade, her history and present position as a world power, is particularly vulnerable to outside influences. It has been said that government today is dictated not by political ideals but by events. In practice it is by a combination of the two, although there are times when events dictate the order of priorities, if not the decisions to be taken.

Since the beginning of this century, successive governments have taken increasing responsibility for social justice and the provision of good minimum living standards for everyone. Britain has one of the world's best welfare states and the same goes for her system of education. The provision of these and other services has meant greater government intervention in all spheres, for, as with the law, in order to provide greater protection, there is some loss of liberty and personal freedom.

State responsibility
In addition to achieving economic security and progress, the government must ensure the protection and security of the country, preserve law and order and pass legislation to protect the majority against the few. It is required to provide social security services and benefits to ensure the minimum standard of living already referred to, and, as far as possible, equality of opportunity for all. Other activities to which it is committed are the provision of consular and diplomatic services, the Foreign Office through which it maintains relations with other countries, management of and payment of interest payments on the national debt, and the granting of aid to underdeveloped countries. Inherent in all this is its administration and cost. In administering its policies and collecting revenue, the government (and its departments) affects every firm, organisation and individual to a greater or lesser extent.

We are concerned here with government intervention in the business world. It can be divided into three spheres:

1. its direct effect on firms through taxation and legislation;
2. its assistance to businesses;
3. its role as an entrepreneur, user and supplier of goods and services through public enterprise.

We must consider these three areas briefly in order to see how the government affects business directly and indirectly, and the interrelationship of state and private activity in commerce and industry.

Taxation

Taxation is the government's main source of revenue. A tax is a compulsory charge levied on the taxpayer by the state. There are two main types of taxation in this country, namely direct and indirect. Income tax, corporation tax, capital transfer tax, motor vehicle tax and local rates are all direct taxes, since they are paid by the taxpayer direct to the respective government department. Indirect taxes are those paid on the purchase or importation of certain goods and services. They include value added tax, customs duties and excise duties. They are indirect because they are paid initially by the manufacturer, importer or wholesaler and then passed on to the final customer.

Taxation can obviously be classified again into three groups: taxes on income, taxes on capital and taxes on expenditure.

While the main function of taxation is to provide revenue, it also has important subsidiary functions and is one of the ways in which the government effects its policies. The first of these is to reduce the inequality of incomes. This has been achieved—and is still being maintained—by income tax and inheritance tax. These taxes are progressive. The amount people pay is in accordance with what they can afford, so that a person with a high income pays more income tax than one who earns less and, in addition, account is taken of their financial responsibilities. Consequently, if two men receive the same amount in wages but one is single and the other is married, the single person will pay more income tax. This system is operated by giving allowances and reliefs against income. Income tax and capital transfer tax (which replaced estate duty) have, therefore, been the main causes of the more equal distribution of Britain's wealth, particularly since the end of the Second World War.

The second subsidiary function of taxation is to control the level of economic activity. Selective employment tax fell into this category, since it encouraged economy in the use of labour in the service and construction industries. The repayment of the tax, together with additional sums to manufacturing industries in the development areas, was an added incentive to firms to move to those areas and therefore stimulated economic activity in them. Similarly, a substantial increase in corporation tax could cause firms to limit their plans for development and expansion, while a reduction in the rate charged would encourage firms to adopt an expansionist policy.

Taxation's third subsidiary function is to influence production and consumption. The imposition of a tax when goods are bought, or excise duty on certain goods, can reduce the total consumption of them. The imposition of tariffs on imported goods will discourage people from buying them and stimulate the sales of home-produced goods. This was one of the measures used at the end of the 1960s to help to correct the balance of payments.

The last two functions can obviously have a direct effect on businesses, while the first will have indirect consequences for them. The effects of taxation are obviously taken into account as far as possible when planning company policy. Companies are subject to corporation tax on their profits and any capital gains obtained by the disposal of assets. The rate of this tax is subject to change in each budget. It is payable to the Inland Revenue.

Besides being subject to taxation themselves, businesses are also responsible for deducting income tax from the wages and salaries of their employees and transmitting it to the Inland Revenue. Wages departments also deduct National Insurance contributions from employees' pay. This is, in effect, another tax, since it represents a compulsory cost to the firm.

The government's financial policy—and hence taxation—is reviewed annually in the budget. Tax changes can be made at other times if they become necessary but changes outside the budget are exceptional. In preparing the budget the Chancellor of the Exchequer must consider the total obligation for government expenditure on education, defence, social services, housing, etc. and decide how this is to be raised. It must be decided how much of this can be raised from taxation; the remainder is financed by borrowing. It is here that the effects of the various forms of taxation must be considered and the right ones chosen for the state of the economy.

A constant watch is kept on levels of employment in all parts of the country, trends of production, prices and the balance of payments throughout the year, by the Chancellor's economic advisors. On the basis of this information the budget is prepared. Work continues constantly on possible taxation changes and their effect and implementation. Major tax reforms require years of work before they can be introduced. However, an effective budget must be designed to suit the *current* economic circumstances of the country. Specific work on it, therefore, begins a few months before Budget Day which usually precedes the beginning of the financial year, which begins on 6 April.

Legislation

The first important sphere of legislation which affects businesses is that relating to contracts. The laws of contract form the framework and security within which firms operate.

Legislation affects the firm in a wide range of its activities: from its formation, when it is subject to the Companies Acts and other respective laws as seen in Chapter 4, to its cessation, for if a firm is doing badly and has to cease trading, the Insolvency and Bankruptcy Acts apply.

The Fair Trading Act 1973 also empowers the Director General of Fair Trading to maintain a continuous review of consumer affairs and take action against traders whose activities affect customers unfairly. The Director General of Fair Trading is responsible for ensuring the enforcement of all legislation relating to consumers' interests, including matters connected with food, description and performance of goods, weights and measures and the safety of goods.

The Factories Act 1961, Offices, Shops and Railway Premises Act 1963 and Health and Safety at Work Act 1974, compel employers to provide minimum standards of safety, hygiene, heating, ventilation, etc. The Redundancy Payments Act provides for those made redundant. The Employment Protection Act gives the employee the right to payment when work is not available (except when this is as a result of a trade dispute) and protects him against unfair dismissal.

On the making and marketing of goods more legislation applies. First, there is that designed to protect the consumer. Manufacturers are required to state the weight and ingredients clearly on their products. The Trade Descriptions Act 1968 imposes penalties on those who mislead the public by false or misleading descriptions of products or their prices.

The Consumer Credit Act 1974 provides protection for those buying goods on credit or hire-purchase and requires businesses involved in these contracts to be licensed.

Legislation exists to examine and, if necessary, control or prevent a monopoly which is considered harmful or against the public interest. Whereas earlier statutes, such as the Monopolies and Mergers Act 1948, had applied only to the private sector, the Competition Act 1980 gave the Monopolies and Mergers Commission responsibility for investigating public sector organisations referred to it by the Secretary of State or the Director General of Fair Trading. Proposed mergers are subject to this procedure when the result of merging would be to create a monopoly or an increase in monopolistic power, or if gross assets would exceed £15,000,000. All aspects of an industry's operations may be investigated. Besides the likely repercussions of a monopoly, costs, services provided and efficiency are all examined. The government has stated its intention of carrying out detailed investigations of nationalised industries as a matter of policy.

There are, besides, many laws and regulations relating to the export of goods. Similarly, imports are subject to various restrictions. Some require licences and quotas before they can enter the country and, of course, duty must be paid on them.

A firm's expansion is also subject to intervention. A company wishing to extend its premises must first obtain planning permission. It is unlikely that this will be forthcoming for heavily industralised areas, but the government will give the firm encouragement and financial help to build in one of the areas which it has nominated for development.

Firms in private enterprise are also subject to other less specific legislation—for example that relating to the hours and conditions of work for drivers of commercial vehicles. The introduction of decimal currency and a metric system involved heavy expenditure for many British firms.

State assistance to businesses
This can be divided into physical or financial help and the provision of information.

Practical assistance is given to firms which move to development areas in the form of investment grants, financial aid with training new staff and providing homes for existing employees who move with the firm, and many other inducements. The training schemes operated by the Department of Employment assist industry and commerce generally as does the work of its employment service in finding labour. The conciliation machinery of the department gives valuable assistance in the field of industrial relations and the settling of disputes. The Industrial Training Boards, too, give direct help in the payment of grants to firms for the training of employees. (Firms also have to pay a levy to these boards.)

Subsidies are paid to agriculture in the form of guarantee payments so that farmers receive a guaranteed price for much of their produce. The state also assists agriculture in other ways.

The Department of Trade and Industry conducts research and encourages the use of advanced techniques in industry. It also gives finance and guidance to small firms and those involved in industries regarded as important to the country, such as computer technology and tourism.

Help with and sponsorship of research which is likely to lead to inventions and/or benefit the public is given through the National Research Development Corporation which is an independent body under the responsibility of the Department of Trade and Industry. Hovercraft and computer projects are among those which were sponsored in this way.

Education, of course, provides an indirect service to industry and commerce in the provision of its future labour force and assists directly by offering training courses in technical colleges.

Financial assistance available to firms through Finance for Industry Limited has already been discussed in Chapter 5.

Information services
The government departments provide very valuable assistance to industry in this sphere. The Department of Trade and Industry provides a wide range of information on various aspects of home and foreign trade. The Export Intelligence Branch collects information about markets all over the world and regularly publishes handbooks describing the services it provides. An important source of current information is the journal *British Business* and the Export Services Bulletin.

The *Employment Gazette* and the *Monthly Digest of Statistics* are also valuable publications and one must not forget the importance of government White Papers.

The government as an entrepreneur, user and supplier of goods and services
The state is a producer in its own right and therefore a direct participator in British industry, through the operation of the nationalised

industries. Collectively these industries employ about one in ten of the working population and are the country's largest employers of labour. In addition, those working in the Civil Service are directly employed by the state. The government, therefore, has an important role to play as an employer and can to some extent affect the level of employment by this means alone.

In order to produce goods and services the public corporations must use the products and services of other organisations in the same way as privately owned firms do. In this way they place important contracts for supplies and equipment. Most of the raw materials for many of them obviously come from state-owned enterprises but machinery and other capital equipment is supplied by privately owned concerns. Contracts for the erection of buildings and plant also go to firms in the private sector. Stationery and other everyday supplies are required in large quantities, and services, from the maintenance of equipment to the cleaning of windows, are needed. Through these orders public corporations can affect the level of activity and employment in other firms and industries. All these industries and the government departments use newspapers and other media for advertising. The government also uses the purchasing power of the public sector to help industry to improve its efficiency.

In some industries the government has a dominant effect as a major customer. It is the main purchaser of drugs and pharmaceutical products, for example, for use in hospitals and other sections of the health service. It also controls the sale of these products as it does those of alcohol. Its vehicles, too, are purchased from firms in private enterprise. Orders from the state airlines form a vital part of the trade of several producers of aircraft. In fact, the aircraft industry is dependent on the government for support. Both it and the Atomic Energy Authority receive financial aid from the state. In these instances, the government influences the type and price of the goods produced. The levels of activity and prosperity of the firms and industries concerned are considerably affected by increases or decreases in government spending in them.

Other government spending has a direct effect in certain industries and consequent secondary effects on others. The decision to build a new motorway, for instance, means contracts for building firms for which they need to engage labour. Orders to their suppliers for raw materials result. The wages paid to those working on the project are used mainly to buy goods and services and, therefore, provide extra trade for other industries. The project, then, is not only providing a motorway with all its benefits, but is also providing additional employment and stimulus to the building industry and the effects of this are multiplied. The current programme for the re-organisation of the shipbuilding industry and consequent grants and loans to firms building ships and engines has attempted to improve its competitiveness in world markets.

All firms are dependent on nationalised industries for the supply of some goods and services. Coal is sold mainly to the gas and electricity authorities, industrial users and individuals for household use. More than half the gas produced is sold for household use and the remainder for industrial and commercial purposes. Coke and other by-products are bought mainly by the chemical industry. A more detailed breakdown of energy resources and the government's role and responsibilities in providing them is given in Chapter 8, under the heading 'Department of Energy'. Industry generally is dependent on iron and steel. Most of these supplies are obtained through the British Steel Corporation which is also responsible for important exports of these products.

Every firm depends to some extent on the transport system, most of which is state-controlled.

Another way in which the government is a direct participator in industry is through its holding of shares in public companies. It is an important shareholder in British Petroleum, for instance.

In 1979 the government placed a number of its British Petroleum shares for public sale with the aim of widening public participation.

During the 1980s it has been government policy to sell off selected nationalised industries, or parts of them, thereby returning them to private ownership. There are plans to extend this policy to other public industries such as gas and electricity.

8

GOVERNMENT DEPARTMENTS WHICH DIRECTLY AFFECT ASPECTS OF COMMERCIAL LIFE

Parliament comprises the House of Commons, the House of Lords and the Queen. Together they form the country's legislative body. Its decisions and policies are executed by the Civil Service at national level, local authorities at local level and the public corporations for the nationalised industries.

The government divides its work and responsibilities into areas or departments. Each is supported by a Civil Service department which is staffed by permanent, paid officials who are servants of the Crown, with a permanent secretary at their head. The function of each department is specialised. The Prime Minister has the power to create new departments and suspend or amalgamate existing ones. The Premier is also responsible for appointing the ministers who are responsible to Parliament for the work of their departments. In this way, the advantages of democracy are complemented by those of continuity and specialised knowledge of work. Ministers come and go but the Civil Service remains. Its continuous life is essential. Ministers depend on its staff for advice.

Government departments, then, collectively cover the whole range of government activity. They are the instruments through which government policy is implemented after the necessary legislation has been passed by Parliament. The entire scope of their work, therefore, alters very little but the way in which it is divided and consequently the responsibility of each department is subject to change. They work in close consultation with local authorities and statutory boards. Although the work of them all affects industry and commerce in varying degrees, many of them have direct and constant contact with organisations in public and private enterprise. Part of the effect and extent of this has already been seen in the last chapter.

The work of the following government departments has a direct impact on all forms of business and consequently brings them into close contact with industry and commerce.

The Department of Trade and Industry

The Secretary of State for Trade and Industry and his department are responsible for promoting British trade and commercial interests abroad and for representing commercial policy and conducting relations with overseas countries. This involves the carrying out of the government's overseas trade policy, negotiation of trade and commercial matters and administration of tariffs. Through the British Overseas Trade Board, the membership of which is appointed by the Secretary of State for Trade and Industry, exports are promoted, and intelligence and information services are provided for all markets. Help, including financial, is given to firms for making overseas visits and to exporters at trade fairs, British weeks and other events abroad.

The provision of information and advice on all aspects of trade with other countries is of particular importance to exporters and those contemplating selling goods or services in foreign markets. It includes assistance with making contacts abroad, and also in dealing with difficulties arising from government regulations here and in the importing country. This help is available from export offices of the Department of Trade and Industry which are situated all over the country.

The department is also concerned with industry and trade at home. It is responsible for administering policy in relation to industry, assisting industry and generally promoting its interests. Thus the department has to develop existing policies and, where necessary, introduce new ones through Parliament. This function and responsibility applies to all manufacturing and service industries in the public as well as the private sector, except for those specifically covered by other departments: the gas and electricity industries, for instance, are the responsibility of the Department of Energy.

The Department of Trade and Industry is, therefore, involved with firms of all sizes, from the very small, to large corporations, such as the Post Office, British Telecom and British Steel. It covers a wide range of interests, from iron and steel and vehicle-manufacturing to tourism and insurance. Its work includes encouraging and promoting information technology, and applying regional policy, with provision of financial assistance. Financial help is also available for small firms, for businesses which are restructuring and for those pursuing programmes of innovation which involve new technology. Help can be obtained from the Department of Trade and Industry by all businesses, in the form of consultation and advice. The implementation of government policy on competition and consumer protection also comes within the responsibility of this department and requires close contact with the Office of Fair Trading and the Monopolies Commission.

The Department of Trade and Industry is responsible for legislation relating to companies. This means ensuring that existing legislation is being followed and initiating new laws when necessary. This responsibility also means that these industries have a direct contact with the government through the Secretary of State for Trade and Industry and can, therefore, discuss problems and make their feeling about particular matters and difficulties known.

The granting of patents, trade marks, and copyrights and the keeping of laws relating to them also come under the wing of this department, as does responsibility for radio frequencies.

The department's journal *British Business* gives valuable statistics and other information about development in all aspects of all trades and industries throughout the country. It also provides an up-to-date picture of activities in the European Community and information on happenings in other countries which may have a bearing on trade and industry in Britain.

Many other government publications are produced regularly, giving valuable information and statistics to industry and commerce on all aspects of trade and economic development.

Department of the Environment

This department is concerned with the physical environment in which we live. It is responsible for administering policies decided by Parliament, for regional planning and development, new towns, the development of cities and the countryside, for water and sewerage, and housing. It must decide on priorities within these policies. Its aim is to ensure the best development of the country's resources.

The department's responsibility for local government concerns all the activities of local authorities, provides their main link with Whitehall and much of their finance. It ensures that the government's housing programme is being fulfilled and deals with plans for the clearance of slums, the development of inner cities as well as the general and overall development of areas.

The planning section of the department is concerned with town and country planning on a national scale and also at a local level. Close liaison is, therefore, required for the designation and development of new towns, and work on town expansion, since several authorities may be involved. Local authorities' plans for the acquisition and disposal of land must have the approval of the Secretary of State before work can commence. The regional economic planning councils and boards have an important part to play here, and also come under the authority of the department. They are advisory bodies which formulate plans for their areas and examine and report on the regional effects of national policies. Local authorities usually consult them before drawing up their proposals for development. This work is important to the location of industry, and well considered development is essential to ensure a fair distribution of the country's wealth.

Department of Transport
A well co-ordinated and efficient transport system is essential to all forms of business. This department has a vital role to play in the planning and development of the country. Every area, every firm and organisation and every individual depends on an efficient transport system and the failure or withdrawal of any one part of it for any length of time causes great difficulties and shortages of goods and supplies.

The Department of Transport is responsible for formulating and developing policies for an integrated internal transport system. This covers three main areas, namely:

1. Nationalised Transport.
2. Highways and Traffic Management.
3. Ports.

Nationalised transport comprises the British Railways Board, the British Waterways Board and the National Bus Company. (The former British Transport Docks Board became privatised as Associated British Ports, and similarly the former National Freight Corporation became a private venture under the name of the National Freight Consortium.) The department appoints the members of these three boards, is responsible for their general policies and management and represents them in Parliament.

The department is responsible for the planning, construction and maintenance of motorways and trunk roads. As we have already seen, this is done in consultation with the Regional Planning and Housing and Local Government sections of the Department of the Environment as well as with Local Government authorities. The Department of

Transport allocates the finance provided by Parliament for expenditure on roads according to the priorities previously decided upon.

An important aspect of the work connected with roads is the management of traffic and study of road safety and its application. In this connection we have the Highway Code and traffic regulations. Continuous research is conducted into the whole question of road safety. Speed limits and the 'breathalyser' laws have already been put into effect, together with legislation on vehicle inspection and testing and on the quality of tyres. The department conducts the Transport and Road Research Laboratory. It handles driver and vehicle licensing and motor taxation, with the assistance of the local authorities.

The whole question of transport is studied by this department for its social benefits and from an economic point of view.

Finally, the department is responsible for the development of ports in peacetime and for their operation in war. In 1983 marine shipping (but not shipbuilding) and civil aviation (but not the aircraft industry or aerospace development) were transferred from the Department of Trade and Industry to the Department of Transport.

Department of Employment
The concern of this department is primarily manpower policy—employment, assistance for the unemployed, creation and preservation of jobs; regional policy and economic planning and their likely effect on employment. It works closely with the Department of the Environment. Obviously, it must have very close contact with industry and the commercial world, as well as with other government departments. It collects and publishes statistics on labour and industrial matters. Employment statistics are published monthly in the journal *Employment Gazette*. The department liaises with the International Labour Office and represents the country on labour and related matters on other international bodies.

Employment
Employment and training services are run through the Manpower Services Commission which comprises a chairman and nine members appointed by the Secretary of State for Employment, in consultation with employers, employees and representatives from education and local government, so that all involved interests are represented. The Commission receives information on local conditions from district manpower committees which exist all over the country. Its general policy

is agreed with the Secretary of State and finance is made available through the Department of Employment by its Employment Service and its Training Services Division.

The main function of the Manpower Services Commission is to assist people to choose, train for, obtain and keep jobs and to help employers to obtain suitable workers. These tasks are carried out by the Employment Service Agency and the Training Services Division.

Employment services.   The Employment Service of the Manpower Services Commission provides a comprehensive service for all those seeking jobs and for employers needing staff. Information and advice on any employment problem is available to anyone who wants it. These services are available throughout the country in Job Centres, where there is a self-service system for discovering job vacancies available and also advice and help from trained personnel, as already mentioned. The larger offices have a Professional and Executive Register for those seeking executive and managerial posts, including scientific and technical appointments. Experienced consultants deal with these vacancies and by access to a computer-based information system, can discover suitable jobs available in any part of the country.

Occupational guidance units provide expert advice on the choice of employment for those who wish to obtain it before selecting a job or changing occupation.

Particular attention is paid by the Department of Employment to helping disabled people obtain and re-train for jobs, through the Disablement Resettlement Service. All employers of twenty or more workers are required to employ some handicapped people. A Register of Disabled Persons is kept and Employment Offices and Job Centres have specially qualified staff who provide vocational guidance, help in finding employment and arrange training where appropriate.

The department is responsible for the issue of work permits to people from abroad who seek employment in this country.

The mobility of labour is obviously desirable and important if an even pattern of employment is to be maintained throughout the country. With the progress of technology, changes in demand, the effect of other market forces and many other factors, unemployment is bound to be heavier in some areas than in others. In an attempt to improve this state of affairs, or prevent its worsening, the Department of Employment implements the government's policy of offering incentives to firms to move to assisted areas or expand in them. It also takes up other schemes to reduce unemployment. This involves giving tax allowances, grants towards the cost of new buildings and equipment and assistance with training personnel. A regional employment subsidy may also be given.

The careers service provided by every local education authority in the country gives vocational and careers advice to young people both in schools and other educational establishments and its own offices, and helps them to obtain jobs. It continues this service during their first years of employment, although they are also free to use the facilities of the Job Centres if they wish.

Training services. The Training Services Division has the task of managing and developing a training programme for the country. This involves co-ordinating, encouraging and building on the training done by employers and filling in the gaps where they exist. The provision of training to enable people to learn and develop skills is important for the individual, and essential to the country in supplying a skilled workforce to industry and contributing to the growth of the economy. It is in an attempt to provide trained people, opportunities for them to make the best use of their skills and to re-train when their original training is no longer relevant that the government has developed a national training programme.

The training opportunities scheme. This scheme (TOPS) is for those over the age of nineteen who wish to acquire a skill, whether it is the first they have learnt or a form of re-training. Training is provided in skill centres, colleges and some firms. Those training under this scheme are paid allowances (varying with the number of dependants) by the Department of Employment.

Many other measures for training young people who are out of work and assisting them to get jobs are carried out in accordance with the Manpower Services Commission's aim of ensuring that 'all young people of sixteen to eighteen years of age who have no job or who are not engaged in further or higher education should have the opportunity of training, of participating in a job creation programme, or of work experience.'

Youth Training Scheme. With unemployment increasing, particularly among the young, the Manpower Services Commission, in conjunction with the Careers Service and local authorities, is continually developing programmes of education and training for the unemployed. As a result, the Youth Training Scheme, as part of a new training initiative, replaced the Youth Opportunities Programme in 1983. It is a comprehensive programme intended to provide a one-year link between school and work for all sixteen-year-olds who require it, and also for those who continued in education after the school-leaving age and are unemployed. The scheme provides work-experience, training related to that work, and education. It is under continuous review, so that it can be strengthened and modified as necessary to meet current needs.

Schemes for the longer-term unemployed, based on projects for community work exist, but are still being developed. They differ from the Youth Training Scheme in that they are not comprehensive. However, the government provides various forms of assistance and encouragement for small firms. These include the new enterprise scheme—in operation in five areas—where unemployed people can receive £40 per week if they start a new business. Job-release, and job-sharing schemes have been introduced to make effective use of existing jobs.

Other functions
The Department of Employment has responsibility for conciliation and arbitration and appoints the members of the Advisory Conciliation and Arbitration Service (ACAS), which is an independent body offering conciliation in industrial disputes to both the public and private sectors of industry and commerce. It also gives advice on all aspects of industrial relations and the management of personnel. The service investigates disputes to discover their causes and suggests remedial action to management and trade unions. Generally, the service is concerned with improving collective bargaining. It investigates complaints of infringement of the rights of individuals under the provisions of legislation, e.g., the Equal Pay Act, 1970 or the Sex Discrimination Act, 1975.

In addition to overseeing the work of the Advisory, Conciliation and Arbitration Service, the Secretary of State for Employment has powers to appoint a court of inquiry or committee of investigation into a dispute where he thinks it is necessary.

Responsibility for health and safety in the work-place rests with the Health and Safety Commission. Its members, drawn from both sides of industry and local authorities, are appointed by the Secretary of State for Employment. Its responsibility is explained by its title. It is generally charged with ensuring that the provisions of the Health and Safety at Work Act, 1974, the Factories Act, 1961, Offices, Shops and

Railway Premises Act, 1963, and those of other relevant legislation are being carried out. At the same time, it develops other measures necessary to ensuring a safe and healthy environment in which to work, while also protecting the general public from industrial hazards.

Department of Education and Science

This department, under the Secretary of State for Education and Science, administers a service which is vital to all sections of the community.

It is responsible for all aspects of education in England and Wales, together with sport, the arts and civil science for Great Britain. Its work falls into several main divisions, each of which is again subdivided. Specialist branches provide advice and information for education. The department interprets and executes the policies formulated by the government. Responsibility for the operation of these, and the provision of adequate facilities for all forms of education in their areas, is passed to the local education authorities with which the department works in close consultation. Each authority is then free to implement the policies in its own way, to meet the needs, conditions and demands of its area.

The Education Act of 1944 is the blueprint for education and local authorities are bound to implement its provisions. The two most important of these are, first, that full-time education must be provided and is compulsory for all children between the ages of five and sixteen. Secondly, provision must be made for further education. Special schools must be provided for children who are mentally or physically handicapped.

Education falls into three main categories: primary, secondary and further. General stipulations regarding the curriculum are made by the Department of Education and Science, but each school is free to select its own within this broad framework. Mainly because of this freedom, many important developments in teaching methods have been made and are taking place in schools throughout the country, through experiment and research. This system is valuable, since it ensures some control over the standard of education offered throughout the country, and at the same time enables schools to adapt the curriculum to meet the changing needs of young people to fit them for life. Official research and development work on teaching methods and examinations is carried out through the School Curriculum Development Committee and the Secondary Examinations Council. These bodies have replaced the former Schools Council. Liaison between the Department of Education and Science and the schools is provided through Her Majesty's Inspectors who visit and report on educational establishments. They also offer help and advice to teachers.

An important task in an educational system, if it is going to be adequate and efficient, is the provision of sufficient and suitably trained teachers. The department achieves this mainly through the provision of courses in recognised Colleges of Education and University Departments of Education. It lays down minimum standards of entry for intending teachers and requires all who teach in state schools to hold recognised teachers' qualifications which it approves. They are then appointed to posts by local authorities or the managers of individual schools. Teachers' salaries are paid on a national scale and a compulsory superannuation scheme is operated.

Physical conditions are obviously important, and the Department of Education and Science must ensure that every area has adequate school buildings. A national building programme is devised, taking into account need and money available. The requirements of each area are considered and permission to extend, re-build and erect new buildings is given where the needs are greatest. Eighty per cent of the cost of these programmes is met from government funds by the department and the remainder by the local authorities concerned.

There are many other aspects closely connected with or embodied in the educational system with which the department is concerned. Among these is the health of children at school. Children are medically examined through the school health service and any matters which need attention are followed up. This service is provided through consultation between the Department of Education and Science, other government departments and local authorities. The department also makes arrangements for school meals.

Primary and secondary schools cover educational needs up to the age of sixteen and in some cases eighteen. Further education is more complex in content, but falls into the following three main areas.

1. Courses up to first degree level

These courses are offered on a full-time or part-time basis. They include non-vocational and recreational courses as well as those of a vocational nature. They are open to all over the age of sixteen, cover a very wide field of subjects and levels, and are provided by local technical colleges, secondary sixth forms, colleges of further education, colleges of commerce, art, and agriculture, and evening centres.

The industrial training boards, created by the Industrial Training Act of 1964, made an important contribution to this sector of education. As a result, many more people have been able to follow courses on day-release and block-release from their firms.

2. *Adult education*

This term generally refers to non-vocational courses for those over eighteen years of age. They are provided mainly by local educational authorities, extramural departments of universities and voluntary bodies like the Workers' Educational Association.

3. *Higher education*

This sector generally covers courses which start at undergraduate or comparable level. They are provided mainly by universities, polytechnics and colleges of education, although some advanced courses are offered by technical colleges and others in the further education sector. The Open University also falls into this category and offers degree courses to those for whom they were not previously available.

The government provides about 80 per cent of the income for universities in the form of grants, but it does not control them or even deal directly with them. They are administered by the University Grants Committee whose members are appointed by the Secretary of State.

An important part of education is the Youth Service which comes under the general responsibility of the Department of Education and Science. The service is administered by local authorities and voluntary organisations. Financial help is provided by the department and the local education authorities. The establishment of the National Training Centre for Youth Leaders indicates government recognition of the importance of this sphere.

Arts

In its role of promoting the arts, the Department of Education and Science has responsibility for public libraries and the Victoria and Albert Museum. In addition, it gives support to the promotion of music, drama, literature, painting and sculpture and other arts which are not otherwise provided for. Much of this work is done through the

Arts Council of Great Britain whose members are appointed by the Secretary of State for Education and Science.

Science
Civil science is the department's responsibility. It carries out, supports and co-ordinates research which does not clearly fall to the authority of other departments. This activity has strong links with work already well established under the department, since much scientific research and development work is carried on in universities and other educational institutions. The Secretary of State receives advice from the Council for Scientific Policy.

The department divides civil science into five main areas. A research council is in charge of each, namely: the Medical Research Council, Natural Environment Research Council, Social Science Research Council, Science Research Council and the Agricultural Research Council.

Even from this brief review, it is clear that the work of the Department of Education and Science is important, wide and far-reaching.

Educational policy in Britain attempts to provide equal opportunities for all and prepare young people for life. More money is spent on this than on any other single area except social security. It is important that the right standards of education are set and maintained. Education can form attitudes and an awareness of social and moral values, including the realisation of the individual's responsibility to society.

The country depends on the education system for trained and well-educated personnel for all areas of industry and commerce— engineers, scientists, managers, doctors, politicians, etc. They, in their turn, are responsible for the progress and standards of industry, commerce and government which are crucial to the state of the country and, ultimately, the standard of living of its people. To survive financially, Britain must produce goods which are highly competitive with those from abroad in quality and price. To do this she must have experts in all the fields mentioned above and she must encourage research and development.

Department of Health and Social Security

An efficient health service and a comprehensive system of social security are important features of modern Britain. These services have been developed and co-ordinated over hundreds of years. Today their scope is wide and effects far-reaching. The administration of these important services is the function of the Department of Health and Social Security. The payment of benefits and collection of contributions under the National Insurance and Industrial Injuries schemes, constitute a large part of its work. The department operates reciprocal agreements for the provision of health services, compensation for industrial injuries and payment of family allowances which exist between Britain and certain other countries. Concern for standards of health and social conditions generally, the raising of them and the promotion of research, is now international. In this connection, the Secretary of State for Social Services represents the United Kingdom at the World Health Organisation of the United Nations.

The work of the department falls clearly into two spheres, firstly, health and secondly, social security, with a Secretary of State directly responsible for each, under the direction of the Secretary of State for Social Services. The functions of each of these sections are briefly examined below.

Health

The state's responsibility for health is almost limitless. It includes all aspects. For simplicity, this responsibility can be divided under two main headings; first public health, which includes drafting and carrying out legislation on the safety of food, control and prevention of infectious diseases and other matters affecting the general health of the public; and secondly personal health, namely, that of individuals.

Public health

Recognition of responsibility by the state for the nation's health was first shown by the passing of the Public Health Act of 1848. The areas of state concern and action have developed considerably since then. The present framework is provided by the Public Health Acts of 1936, 1961 and 1968. The disposal of refuse and sewerage, provision for the cleaning of streets and a supply of pure water are important functions of this department. Its activities also include the abatement of noise and certain responsibility for the control of pollution. The Public Health administration aims to provide and maintain conditions conducive to a high level of health for the whole community. Anything likely to affect this is, therefore, its concern. Its prime task is to establish conditions to promote and ensure hygiene and the control of infection and disease. Its activities include investigating, improving and operating means of prevention. Comprehensive legislation exists on the description of food and purity or safety of its ingredients, and the safety of conditions in which it is prepared and handled. Places where food is prepared or sold must conform to specified standards of hygiene and are examined to ensure that these are met.

Most public health activities are carried out by the local authorities, with which the Department of Health and Social Security works closely.

Since it is important to aim continually to improve standards of health, research is vital. This, too, is undertaken by the department.

Personal health

The National Health Service is all-embracing in its concern with every aspect of the health of the individual, and it is available to everyone.

The National Health Service Act 1946 introduced the health service in its present form. Its aim was to provide all kinds of medical attention for those who need it, without exception. It includes the hospital services (both general and specialist) which are operated through the regional boards and management committees. The family doctor and dentist provide the public's most constant contact with the service, as do pharmacists and opticians.

Health and welfare services provided by the local authorities have an important role in care and personal health and are therefore the responsibility of the Department of Health and Social Security but administered by local councils. They include a wide variety of services for mothers and young children, from all forms of maternity care to the provision of clinics and health visitors who visit homes and give advice and medical attention to babies, mothers and young children. Welfare foods are also available at reduced prices. Responsibility for children in need of care falls to this department, but most of the services are provided through local authorities.

Home nursing, domestic help and other services for the elderly are provided by local authorities under the National Health Service. Treatment and care for the mentally and physically handicapped are also made available at local level.

Social security

This century has seen an increasing concern by the state for the social needs of the population.

A comprehensive system of social security is operated in Britain. It has been developed gradually over a very long period and covers a wide area, from old age pensions to supplementary benefits. Co-ordination of all services was provided by legislation which came into force in 1948. Several additions and amendments have been made since. The aim is to cover, as far as possible, all needs and ensure an adequate basic standard of living for all.

Child benefit payments are paid to families, for all children below the age of sixteen (nineteen in the case of those remaining at school or undertaking apprenticeships). Sickness benefit is paid to employed persons who are away from work because of illness. Under the indus-trial injuries insurance scheme, benefits are paid to those who are injured in accidents caused by or occurring in the course of employ-ment. Similarly, payments are made to those who contract named diseases caused by the nature of their work. Disablement and invalidity benefit is paid in certain cases, as is death benefit to dependants, in some circumstances. Pensions are paid to widows. Unemployment benefit is available for those out of work.

A long-standing and important part of the social services, is provision for the elderly, to whom retirement pensions are paid—to men over sixty-five and women over sixty years of age.

A comprehensive system of supplementary benefits was introduced by the Ministry of Social Security Act 1966, which replaced and widely extended the previous scheme of national assistance. Its provisions extend to all over the age of sixteen who are not in full-time employ-ment or education (and not involved in trade disputes) and have in-sufficient means to meet their demands. Payment is calculated according to personal responsibility and circumstances, and made through employment exchanges of the Department of Employment. This is another illustration of two government departments working in close co-operation with each other.

Other allowances and benefits are payable to those injured during war or service in the armed forces, and to their dependants. A welfare service gives advice and assistance to war pensioners and their dependants.

Further services, in addition to those mentioned here, are provided by the Department of Health and Social Security. It is obvious that its area of responsibility is very wide, and important to realise that its services are under constant review since, to be effective, they must meet the continually changing needs of society.

Finance for health and social security benefits comes from national insurance contributions, which are paid by all employed and self-employed persons and their employers each week, from Exchequer funds and some local authority money.

It can be clearly seen that the whole range of social services is interconnected by being the responsibility of one department. This is the only way to achieve an effective and comprehensive system. It is also essential, as can be seen from this brief review, that the department works closely with other government departments and local authorities.

Department of Energy
The department carries out government policy on energy resources. It is responsible for the National Coal Board, the Electricity Council and the Central Electricity Generating Board, the British Gas Corporation, the United Kingdom Atomic Energy Authority, and the British National Oil Corporation. The Secretary of State for Energy is Chairman of the Nuclear Power Advisory Board. It shares regional offices with the Department of Industry.

Analysis of responsibilities:

Civil Emergency Planning Unit
The unit is the focal point in the department for dealing with civil emergencies arising in or affecting the department's industries.

Atomic Energy Division
Financing of Atomic Energy Authority. Government relationship with British Nuclear Fuels Ltd and Amersham International. Sponsorship of nuclear design and construction industry. International aspects of atomic energy, including UK participation in IAEA, NEA and Euratom.

Coal Division
Policy relating to the coal industry, including administration of the Coal Industry Acts, NCB borrowings and investment. General liaison with the coal distributive trade. Authorisation of NCB open-cast workings. Mining subsidence.

Community and International Policy Division
Policy relating to international and European Community energy and oil matters.

Economics and Statistics Division
Provision of statistical reports, forecasts and analyses on energy.

Electricity Division
Policy relating to the electricity supply industry in England and Wales, including statutory structure of the industry. Administration of Electricity Supply Acts and the Electricity Acts. Electricity industry borrowing, investment and prices. Accident investigation and meter examination.

Energy and Nationalised Industry Policy Division
Development of nationalised industry energy policy.

Energy Technology Division
Provision of scientific and technological support and advice on the energy sector of the economy, and on the iron and steel industry. Supports divisions dealing with fuel policy, fuel and power industries, Atomic Energy Authority, and iron and steel industry.

Gas Division
Policy relating to the gas industry. Administration of the Gas Act 1972. British Gas Corporation borrowings, investment and prices. Pricing of Continental Shelf gas. Safety measures for distribution and use of gas. Accident investigation and gas quality and meter examination.

Mines and Quarries Inspectorate
Ensures observance both below and above ground of the acts and regulations on safety and health of people and the care and treatment of horses in mines and quarries. Inspectors investigate accidents and dangerous occurrences, attend inquests, initiate action to ensure compliance with the law, and advise on matters affecting health, safety and training.

Nuclear Installations Inspectorate
Regulation of safety of nuclear power stations, nuclear-fuel processing plants, research reactors and isotope-manufacturing plants licensed by the department under the Nuclear Installations Act.

Offshore Supplies Office
Promotion and development of the UK's oil and gas resources. Enabling the UK to compete effectively in the supply of goods and

services for offshore oil and gas developments in UK waters and worldwide. Also other follow-up of the IMEG Report. Sponsorship of industries involved in offshore supplies that are not covered elsewhere in the department.

Oil Policy (Home) Division
Home oil policy, refineries and stockpiling, long-term emergency planning. Prices, finances of UK oil companies, administration of Pipelines Act 1962.

Oil Policy (Overseas) Division
Overseas oil policy, world crude oil supply, demand and transport and security of supplies, pricing.

Petroleum Production Division
Licensing policy and legislation. Safety regulations, off-shore pollution. Assessment of discoveries and reserves, supervision of production.

Safety and Health Division
Administration of Mines and Quarries Act, etc.; third-party liability in the field of Nuclear Energy (Nuclear Installations Acts).

9

LOCAL GOVERNMENT

Local government plays a very important part in the lives of all of us and greatly affects business. Collectively it employs over two million people and spends something approaching £35,000 million a year. Its functions range from registering births and deaths to arranging for refuse to be collected.

Organisation

The organisation of local government is similar to that of Whitehall. The same democratic principles are applied. People resident in each area elect councillors to represent them in local affairs, through their membership of district and county councils. They constitute the legislature and decision-making body at local level, just as Members of Parliament, the elected representatives in national affairs, constitute the House of Commons which formulates policy and makes laws for the whole country.

The decisions made by local councils, whose members work voluntarily, are passed on to the various local government officers and administered by their departments in the local council house or town hall. These are full-time permanent, paid officials. Like that of the central government the work of local authorities is divided into departments which have the advantages of continuity and specialist knowledge. Councillors, on the other hand, are elected for a stated period of office and their appointment is unpaid.

Councillors work part time and though they receive no salary are entitled to certain allowances when they attend council meetings and carry out other necessary duties.

The present structure of local government dates from 1 April 1974, when a major reorganisation took place. The previous system was old and consequently the size and authority of its units varied considerably, from county and county borough councils to parish councils. There was considerable variation even in the size of each type of unit. The population has increased considerably since Victorian times when the system was established. In addition, local authorities today are expected to provide a higher standard of service (made possible by technical and scientific developments) and a wider range of services.

Under the present two-tier system, the whole of England and Wales (except Greater London) is divided into fifty-nine counties. Each of these has its own county council which is responsible for the larger-scale services provided by local government, such as planning and administration over wide areas and those requiring substantial resources. These include strategic planning, police and fire services, education, libraries, highways, traffic regulations and refuse disposal.

District authorities, of which there are 369, comprise the second tier of local government. They are responsible for functions which have a strong local element and require knowledge of the area, its problems and needs. For example, they deal with environmental health, housing, refuse collection and make decisions on planning applications. Some functions, such as the supervision of parks and museums, are carried out by both tiers, who reach an agreement on what services are needed and how they are to be provided.

Six of the largest counties which cover the main industrial centres of the country, with their large urban developments and population, are called metropolitan counties. They are:

Greater Manchester	Tyne and Wear
Merseyside	West Midlands
South Yorkshire	West Yorkshire

These counties (which, with the Greater London Council, may be subject to Parliamentary action) have overall responsibility for making policies and providing services for all the areas within their geographical net, in the same way that the non-metropolitan counties do. However, four services are passed to their second tier, namely the metropolitan districts.These four are:

Education
Personal social services
Careers services
Libraries.

The reason is that the greater size of the metropolitan districts, with their substantial population and funding, allows them to provide these services more efficiently than the non-metropolitan districts, which contain far fewer people.

In practice, each household has some services provided by its district council and others by its county council, and elects councillors to both councils. The table below shows how the local government services are divided between county and district authorities.

Fig. B	Metropolitan*		Non-Metropolitan	
	Counties	Districts	Counties	Districts
Large-scale planning Roads and traffic Road safety Parking Highway lighting Police Fire service	▓		▓	
Education Personal social services Youth employment Libraries		▓	▓	
Local plans Planning applications Housing House improvement grants Slum clearance Environmental health Refuse collection Rent rebates Rates and rate rebates		▓		▓

Source: Department of the Environment and the Welsh Office booklet.
  Pub. Central Office of Information.
  *See page 86.

The functions of local government
The services which are provided and administered by local authorities have altered very little in the latest structural changes, but the names of the departments responsible for some of them have changed slightly and, as already seen above, they are divided between county and district councils on a uniform national basis.

The first duty of local councils is to administer the policies and legislation of the government. All their powers come from Parliament and can be changed by it. This is shown by the major changes in the structure of local government itself, already referred to. Much government policy, then, is implemented through the local authorities which, in their turn, have the authority to enforce it. The government's decision to re-organise education on comprehensive lines, for instance, put an obligation on local authorities to draw up plans for the introduction of the system in their areas and submit them to the Department of Education and Science for official approval. This also demonstrates the interaction of government machinery at national and local level.

The second duty of local authorities is the administrative one of managing the affairs of the area and providing services in the best interests of the inhabitants.

The manager and chief of a local authority is the Chief Executive. He co-ordinates the work of departments to avoid duplication and overlapping. As clerk or secretary to the council, he is able to provide a vital link between it and the local government departments. Consequently, he has first-hand knowledge of the decisions made at council meetings and of the progress of each of the full-time departments. He liaises closely with central government departments and with the chief executives of other counties and districts. He must be a good administrator and, to do the job well, have energy and drive and the ability to get on well with people.

The easiest way to see the work of a local authority is to study the functions of some of the main departments. The following exist in a metropolitan district:

Finance department
This is a local authority's exchequer and is responsible for the collection of revenue and the payment and receipt of expenditure. It is headed by a Director of Finance.

Revenue from all sources is paid to this department. This includes payment of rates, and receipt of the annual government grant, which are the two main sources of income, together with any revenue from trading by the authority. The last source will include rent from houses and any other property owned by the authority, and from other sources like swimming pools, entertainment facilities, car parks, etc. With the finance committee of the council, the Director of Finance and his department decide the amount of the rate to be levied and the extent of any borrowing which may be considered necessary. The department pays wages and salaries to all local government employees. It is responsible for making payments to the other departments according to the decisions for the allocation of money made by the council. Detailed accounts must be kept of all transactions, together with a system of budgetary control.

Among its responsibilities is that for making advances to individuals for house purchase, and the management of funds invested, such as superannuation contributions.

The Finance Department is naturally in close contact with every other local government department and with other organisations which deal with them.

Technical Services Department

The Director of Technical Services and his department are responsible for local planning generally and to ensure that the requirements of the Town and Country Planning Acts and other relevant legislation are met. They must work in close consultation with the county council, all the bodies concerned with regional planning and, of course, the Department of the Environment.

Private plans for new buildings, and those for changes and additions to existing ones, must be submitted to the Director of Technical Services for approval. All buildings owned by the district authority are the responsibility of this department. It is the duty of the director and his staff to maintain and repair them. Painting and decorating of schools, libraries and civic buildings is, therefore, carried out by them.

The important responsibility for planning new roads and bridges and maintaining existing ones, together with that for providing traffic signs, public lighting, footpaths and other activities related to road safety, lies with the county. In practice, however, the Director of Technical Services in a district has close contact with the county authority and, in fact, often carries out much of this work in his area under the control and at the request of the county.

Department for Environmental Health

The Director of Environmental Health and his department are concerned with promoting and preserving the good health of the inhabitants of an area. Environmental factors—such as ensuring adequate standards of housing by preventing over-crowding, demolishing slum property and re-accommodating those involved —are important in any area. The Director of Environmental Health or Chief Environmental Health Officer, as he is more commonly called, is responsible for these measures under the provisions of the Public Health Act, 1936, and additional guidance or directives issued by the Department of the Environment. Measures of this kind are taken only after close consultation with the Housing Manager in his department.

The control of air pollution and noise, the inspection of shops (and other premises where food is handled for the public) to ensure hygiene, make an important contribution to the preservation of good health. Pest control is another valuable service provided by this department. Its inspections of offices, shops and railway premises, under the provisions of the 1963 Act, bring the chief officer and his staff into close contact with firms in its area.

Education Department

In most areas education accounts for the largest amount of expenditure. It comprises primary, secondary and special schools and further education. This involves providing and maintaining schools and other necessary buildings. Details of building requirements have to be submitted to the Department of Education and Science, which then determines their size and cost in accordance with its national programme.

School meals and any other necessary materials and supplies must be provided. This means contact with many firms and organisations. Close liaison with the area health authority is needed to provide the medical inspections and treatment required by law.

Other work includes the provision of a youth service, educational research, and making grants available to students. A Careers and Employment service is also provided by each local education authority and includes vocational guidance. The Careers Service in each area works closely with the Manpower Services Commission, and in particular with its Training Services Division. The latter is responsible for putting into operation the wide range of measures devised to provide opportunities for people to acquire new skills and training.

A library service, both fixed and mobile, is usually the responsibility of a special section of the Education Department.

Social Services Department

General social services, under a director, are the responsibility of metropolitan districts and non-metropolitan counties. An important aspect of this work is the care of children who have no parents, or who are being badly treated at home, and those committed to care by the Juvenile Court. This is done under the guidance of a Children's Officer, who looks after the children in all respects. Homes are provided by the authority and voluntary bodies. Children are placed with foster parents and a watchful eye is kept on them to ensure their safety and care. This department also supplies a wide range of welfare services for the old, physically handicapped, blind and others in need of help or accommodation permanently or temporarily. Many voluntary associations offer valuable help in many spheres, such as staffing day centres and providing meals-on-wheels. The Social Services Department is also partly responsible for setting up adult training centres for those who suffer from some handicap which prevents, or makes difficult for them, training in the usual establishments for further education or with a firm.

Housing Department

This department provides council houses and flats and approves grants for the conversion or improvement of privately owned property. It works closely with the Technical Services Department, since the latter is responsible for carrying out the actual repairs and maintenance work. It also works closely with the Social Services Department in providing homes for the old, handicapped and others in need, and with the Chief Environmental Health Officer and his staff on projects for slum clearance, re-housing and similar work.

It has already been shown that under the present organisation of local government, responsibility for large-scale planning which affects a wide area—for roads, traffic and road safety, the provision of police and fire services—lies with the counties in both metropolitan and non-metropolitan areas. However, from the brief description of services provided at district level given above, it is clear that much consultation and co-operation exists between each county and the districts in its area, so that services are made available in the best and most efficient way.

Law and order are maintained locally through the police force and the courts. In fact, the police are now controlled by a special authority of the county council and the magistrates. Protection against fire is given by the fire services by means of a fire brigade. Inspections of premises are made to ensure that there are adequate means of prevention, escape and exit, and that sufficient precautions are taken in all buildings used by the public or where people are employed. These services, too, are provided at county level, as are those of the Weights and Measures Departments, which now have increased responsibility for consumer protection.

Citizens' Advice Bureaux have been set up all over the country to assist people and acquaint them with all the services provided by local government, central government and other bodies.

Income

A local authority's income comes mainly from rates, which are a local tax levied on privately owned property, business and industrial premises; central government grants which are made annually; and revenue from its own trading.

The last source of money includes rents from houses and other property owned by the council, and income from swimming pools and other recreational facilities, as already mentioned in this chapter. Letting of the town or civic hall and assembly rooms for private functions provides an income for many authorities. Dividend and interest are received on investments, and ground rent from land owned by the council. The supply of water also yields income.

Many local authorities, particularly those in holiday resorts, receive income from entertainment facilities and other amenities provided. Birmingham operates its own bank.

The importance of the work of local government departments to businesses in their area is obvious. In addition, large contracts for the building of a shopping centre, housing estate or recreation centre, for example, can stimulate the activity of an area. Orders for supplies required for the work of the various departments also bring important business to firms. Loans to local authorities provide a safe investment and income for businesses and private individuals.

Note

The Metropolitan Counties were abolished on 1 April 1986. Residuary Bodies were appointed by the Secretary of State for the Environment to wind up and hand over their work to District Councils and some to County Councils. This introduces a uniform two-tier system of local government throughout the country.

A notable exception to this simplification is the Inner London Education Authority, which retains its identity and control over a large part of the capital's education system. Previously a part of the Greater London Council, it has survived as an independent body with its own elected council and finances.

10

PUBLIC CORPORATIONS

The British government is a direct participator in industry and a direct employer of labour, through the nationalised industries.

During the last quarter of the nineteenth century it was widely felt that some state intervention in certain spheres was necessary in the interests of the community. This was in direct contrast to the laissez-faire (leave alone) policy which had been in operation for many years.

The first of the modern examples of public corporations was the formation of the Port of London Authority in 1908. In 1937 the British Broadcasting Company became the British Broadcasting Corporation. The Central Electricity Board was formed in 1933 and followed in 1939 by the British Overseas Airways Corporation, since changed to British Airways.

The 1930s were overshadowed by the depression and trade slump, followed in 1939 by the outbreak of the Second World War. There was a coalition government whose time, energy, and money were all absorbed by the demands of the war, so the question of nationalisation was shelved. In 1945 a Labour government under Clement Attlee was elected and a drive towards nationalisation resulted. The Bank of England, the coal industry, British European Airways and British South American Airways were all nationalised in 1946, and the British Overseas Airways Corporation recommenced operations. The British Transport Commission was formed in 1947 with responsibility for roads and railways. Electricity was nationalised in the same year with administration on a regional basis under the central control of the British Electricity Authority. Gas, too, was nationalised in 1948; the country was divided into twelve areas, each with a gas board, under the central control of the Gas Council. Finally, iron and steel were nationalised in 1949. The Independent Television Authority, set up in 1954, is another nationalised body.

In 1951 a Conservative government was returned to power with its policy of private enterprise. As a result, road transport and iron and steel were de-nationalised in 1953. A year later, however, atomic energy was nationalised under the Atomic Energy Authority. Because of the special characteristics of the industry, the danger and importance of atomic energy, the secrecy of the work and the large amounts of money required, it was felt that in the interests of the country it should be under state control.

A Labour government was returned to power in 1964. During its administration the steel industry was re-nationalised.

The Conservative government which came to power in 1979, and was re-elected in 1983, has favoured private enterprise and sold off several firms which were previously nationalised. Amersham International was one of these and, therefore, became a public limited company. In 1981, British Aerospace was changed into a public limited company when just over 51 per cent of its shares were sold to the public while the government retained 48.43 per cent of them. There are plans to extend this policy of privatisation by selling some complete industries to the private sector, but also by selling off particular parts of nationalised industries—one example is British Telecom—thereby introducing private capital into what has previously been public enterprise and, consequently, introducing or increasing competition.

What is nationalisation?

Nationalisation is the taking over of an industry or enterprise by the state, in terms of ownership and control. A nationalised industry is created by Act of Parliament which confers its powers and assets on a statutory body, usually a public corporation, and lays down its organisation, functions and powers. This body is under a considerable but varying degree of ministerial control.

There are two main alternatives available for the organisation of a nationalised industry. The first is direct state control through a government department, with a minister in charge of each industry, like the ministerial system used for welfare and social services. The second is control through an authority appointed by the government. The second method is the most popular method in Britain. Most of the nationalised industries are run by public corporations set up by and answerable to Parliament. The Post Office, however, Britain's oldest state-owned industry, was organised as a government department until 1970, when it became a public corporation.

The government obtains ownership by taking over the shares of the companies in question. To do this it pays compensation to the shareholders, the amount being decided by the market price of the shares at a certain date some time before the decision to nationalise was taken.

The shares then become government stock and bear a fixed rate of interest which is payable regardless of whether a profit or loss is made. This rate is usually between 3½ and 4½ per cent. Former shareholders have the option of retaining their shares as government stock or selling them at the price offered. In most cases this is quite generous.

Minister's powers
When the procedure described above is completed state control is achieved. The industry is then placed under the general control of a minister whose duty is to supervise it in a broad sense. He represents it in Parliament and represents Parliament to the industry, thereby maintaining constant contact between the two bodies, but he does not take part in the day-to-day running of the industry. This is left completely to the board or public corporation. The minister must guide and direct the industry on matters of general policy. The actual extent of his control varies from one industry to another, because of the varying and specialised nature of each enterprise. He authorises money for capital through Parliament. Annual reports and accounts must be submitted to Parliament by every nationalised industry.

The minister must ensure that the consumer's interests are catered for and protected. In most cases this is done by setting up a Consumer Council for each industry, which deals with consumers' views and complaints and makes recommendations to the board and the minister.

Public corporations and control
A public corporation is established by the minister in charge of the industry appointing a board which is responsible for the day-to-day running of the industry. It can be compared with the board of directors of a public company. Like the power of the minister, that of the public corporations varies slightly from one to another because of the specialised nature of each industry but each is responsible for the management of its industry and answerable to Parliament.

Each public corporation, like a company, is a corporate body—it has a legal identity and can, therefore, take legal action and have legal action taken against it. It owns assets and must operate them in the public interest. It should be noted that because the nationalised industries are state-owned, holders of government stock in a particular industry have no voting rights. Their ownership of stock gives them no greater claim to the industry, or say in its running, than the rest of the population.

Finance

The main aim of a nationalised industry is to operate in the best interests of the public and the nation as a whole. It must, therefore, combine the aims of providing a good and efficient product or service and of covering its costs. Unlike private enterprise, public corporations do not aim to make a profit. However, most Acts of Parliament which relate to them state that the industries should break even, taking one year with another. This is stated more specifically in the White Paper issued by the government in 1961, following the investigations of the Radcliffe Committee, which requires nationalised industries to break even over a five-year period. Successive White Papers have developed this requirement. Thus there is no truth in the myth that they could make a loss in successive years and be automatically subsidised by the Treasury. Payment of interest and provision for depreciation must be included in the annual figures leading to a surplus or loss. The White Papers also state that money must be set aside for capital development. Each board now has to meet financial targets which the government lays down. These have become more stringent in recent years. They are usually set for three to five years and require the industry to produce a stated return on net assets employed. Each target is set after taking careful account of the particular nature, characteristics and problems of the industry concerned.

In 1980, the government took some of British Gas profits and subsequently reinforced this move by imposing an annual gas levy which, in effect, puts into central government funds a percentage of British Gas profits. This was £383 million in 1981/2. The corporation must still meet its financial target of 3.5 per cent return on net assets employed. Government directive was also responsible for increases in the price of gas for three years—in spite of the corporation's substantial profits—in order to achieve the government's aim of parity of energy prices. In contrast, British Rail made a loss in the region of £87 million in 1982. However, railways are in most countries recognised as loss-makers, but because they provide an important service to the community are subsidised, most of them much more heavily than is the case with the British system.

Surpluses must be ploughed back into the industry or passed on to the consumer in the form of lower prices. During the second half of the 1970s some nationalised industries' prices were held down several times by successive governments to further general government policy against inflation.

Additional capital requirements are met by loans from the government on payment of interest, and occasionally by making new issues of government stock. Short term capital is obtained by bank advances and other means available as used by firms in private enterprise.

Why nationalise?

There are many economic, political and social reasons put forward for nationalising particular industries. Although the question of state control has become very involved in politics, many people would argue that the basic industries already nationalised in this country are better and more fairly operated under state control than they would be under private enterprise.

The main reason for the nationalisation of most industries is to enable them to be run in the best interests of the state economically and socially. State control gives the advantage of a monopoly run in the public interest, and the economies of large-scale production. Co-ordination and rationalisation are possible, so that duplication is largely avoided and planning, development and research can be carried out on a national scale. Because of their size, public corporations are able to attract experts in management, technology and research. Security of employment has helped to promote good labour relations. State ownership ensures the provision of adequate capital which was not available to some industries when they were in private hands. In the interests of national security, nationalisation of certain industries—for exampie, atomic energy—is desirable.

Many arguments are voiced against state control. Perhaps the most notable among them is that of bureaucracy or red tape, and closely allied to it the view that absence of the profit motive breeds apathy and lack of progress. In answer to this it is important to note that throughout the 1960s increases in productivity in the nationalised industries were much greater than in the private sector. The absence of competition is another disadvantage often stated. In fact, in several spheres, while public corporations have the monopoly of their industry, there is an element of competition between them. For example, in the supply of power, there is strong competition between gas and electricity. Lack of control by the public in practice, and political interference as seen particularly in the aviation industry are other common arguments against nationalisation.

Examples of nationalised industries

1. *Coal*

The National Coal Board was formed by the Coal Industry National-isation Act 1946, to carry out all the functions involved in:

(a) working and getting the coal in Great Britain, to the exclusion (save as in this Act provided) of any other person;

(b) securing the efficient development of the coal-mining industry; and

(c) making supplies of coal available, of such qualities and sizes, in such quantities and at such prices, as may seem to them best calculated to further the public interests in all respects, includ-ing the avoidance of any undue or unreasonable preference or advantage. (*Coal Industry Nationalisation Act*, 1946, HMSO).

The board comprises a chairman and from eight to eleven members all of whom are appointed by the Department of Energy. It is respon-sible for the day-to-day operation and management of the industry according to the general policy laid down by the Secretary of State, and is answerable to him.

He represents the industry in Parliament, keeps in touch with the state of the industry and events affecting it, transmits parliamentary policy to the Board, sees that this is followed and the public interest served efficiently. He can issue directives on matters affecting the public and his authority must be obtained before money can be bor-rowed to finance capital investment. Temporary borrowing within limits laid down by Parliament must also have the sanction of the Secretary of State. Most of the industry's capital is obtained in loans from the Treasury.

Responsibility for all aspects of the day-to-day running and man-agement of the whole industry is vested in the National Coal Board. To facilitate more effective and efficient management of the industry the collieries are divided into separate areas with a director in charge of each. They are answerable to the board for the operation of the collieries in their areas. Finally, each colliery or group of collieries has its own manager and organisation structure.

This form of organisation of the industry provides the advantage of centralised thinking and policy which can be applied from an overall view of the industry, so that the most efficient use of resources is made, while attention is still paid to the differing needs and problems of the pits in each area, through the area directors.

Most of the coal pits in the country are operated by employees of the National Coal Board and machinery owned by it, but the board also gives authorisation for the operation of some small pits to firms in the private sector. Apart from supplying large quantities of coal direct to big industrial users, the board leaves the distribution of coal to private enterprise.

Overall demand for coal has declined during the last decade. In fact, with the exception of the demands of the electricity industry which have increased, the quantity of coal required by every other class of consumer has declined in favour of other types of fuel. Consequently, the industry is having to face the problem of running down production and labour requirements. This is being achieved while productivity is increasing.

2. *Gas*

The industry was nationalised by the Gas Act of 1948. As a result the Gas Council was appointed by the then Minister of Power and began its work on 1 May 1949. In 1973 this was replaced by the British Gas Corporation. This body is composed of a chairman and deputy chairman and twelve members. The Corporation's main task is to act as guide and coordinator to the regions. It also raises capital, conducts research and is responsible for preserving good industrial relations in the industry. An important duty is, of course, to keep the Secretary of State for Energy informed of the state of the industry and the problems affecting it. The Gas Act 1965 gave the Corporation extended responsibility for trading by requiring it to produce, or acquire from abroad, sufficient quantities of gas to supply the needs of the area gas boards. Negotiations by the council for purchasing North Sea gas for the whole industry began from this and still continue. However, The Oil and Gas (Enterprise) Act 1982 curtailed the Corporation's monopoly in the supply of gas for fuel by allowing companies in the private sector to compete in this supply.

Responsibility for the distribution of gas for each area is delegated to the respective region. For this purpose, the country is divided into twelve regions, each of which has a large measure of independence. Because the needs of areas vary, each region is free to determine its own organisation and working structure. In practice, the regions purchase quantities of North Sea gas from the British Gas Corporation.

In the era of manufactured gas, the industry was locally-based. This situation has changed totally, following conversion to natural gas, and the industry is now highly centralised like most of the other nationalised industries.

The members of each region as shown in Figure C are appointed by the Secretary of State. They comprise a chairman and deputy chairman who are usually full-time officials, one or more full-time members and several part-time members.

Fig. C

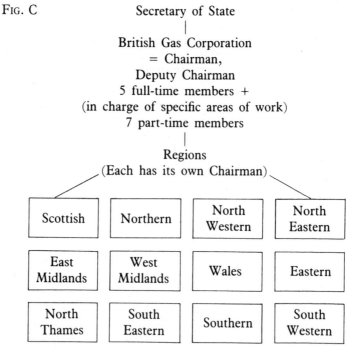

Secretary of State
|
British Gas Corporation
= Chairman,
Deputy Chairman
5 full-time members +
(in charge of specific areas of work)
7 part-time members
|
Regions
(Each has its own Chairman)

Scottish	Northern	North Western	North Eastern
East Midlands	West Midlands	Wales	Eastern
North Thames	South Eastern	Southern	South Western

British Gas is to be privatised in October 1986, when the Government will offer its shares for sale to the public.

3. *British Airways*

Unlike the coal and gas industries, which are completely state-owned, the air transport industry comprises private and public enterprise. British Airways operates side by side and in competition with independent airlines.

The structure, organisation and operation of British Airways are laid down in the Civil Aviation Act, 1971, which amalgamated British European Airways and the British Overseas Airways Corporation and brought British Airways into operation.

The British Airways Board comprises a chairman and up to fifteen members, all of whom are appointed by the Secretary of State for Transport. The function of the Secretary of State is to keep a general eye on the industry, be aware of its current position, problems and difficulties and report on them to Parliament where he is the industry's spokesman. He must be able to see how the state of British Airways and its operations affect the country and, if necessary, give direct general instructions to their board to act in what he and Parliament considers are the best interests of the public. This power is rarely used.

Capital expenditure by the board must be approved by the Secretary of State, who also obtains government loans within the limits laid down by Parliament, and specifies the financial targets they are expected to meet.

Within this framework, the management and running of British Airways is left to the board.

The work of British Airways is conducted by its seven divisions. Collectively these cover long-distance routes, including round-the-world services and regular services to the main centres in Europe, the Americas and the Far and Middle East. Short and medium-haul services inside Britain and to the rest of Europe, North Africa and the Middle East, are provided by the European Division. British Airways also operates domestic services which meet an important social need by making regular contact with the Islands and Highlands of Scotland and other remote parts. Some of these flights are not profitable and, therefore, may not be operated by private enterprise or, if they were, would be at a high cost to the passenger. Its total route network is the largest in the world.

British Airways board owns, or has investments in a number of hotels, owns airlines in different parts of the world and a helicopter division. It has part-ownership in several associated companies which co-operate with it in providing services.

Several independent airline companies operate alongside and, in some cases, in competition with British Airways. Their existence is necessary to ensure the provision of the wide range of services they provide, as well as to cope with the very great expansion in demand for air services both for freight and passenger transport. The main independent company is British Caledonian Airways which was formed in 1970 by the merger of Caledonian Airways and British United Airways.

The Civil Aviation Act 1980 provides the legislation necessary for the government to change British Airways from a nationalised industry to a public limited company. The act makes it possible to offer shares for sale to private investors.

Summary

Comparison of private enterprise and nationalised industries
The nationalised industry exists for the public good and is concerned with providing a service as well as making ends meet. The primary aim of the firm in private enterprise, on the other hand, is to make a profit. The provision of a service is of secondary importance.

The board of directors of a company is elected by its shareholders and is responsible to them. A public corporation is answerable to Parliament through a minister who chooses its members. The shareholders of a company are its owners and, therefore, have a say in its running and receive a share of its profits. The state owns nationalised industries. Holders of stock in them receive a fixed rate of interest, irrespective of the state of the industry, and have no say in its running. Any remaining profit is ploughed back into the industry or used to reduce the price of the product or service to the consumer. In private enterprise this is issued to the shareholders in the form of dividend.

Inherent in the comparisons just made are differences in attitude. The main aim of the nationalised industry is to provide a service. Although it has to pay attention to costs, they and profits are not its only considerations. Electricity, for example, is supplied to remote parts of the country where the cost of bringing it is greater than the price paid by the people using it. If the industry were in private hands the receivers would have to pay the full economic price for electricity.

Internal organisation and job structure and pay in a nationalised industry are less flexible than in firms in private enterprise. There is now an emphasis on greater flexibility within state-controlled concerns, however.

11

BANKING

Origin

The goldsmiths of the seventeenth century were the first real English bankers.

Gold and silver were accepted internationally for the payment of debts. Gold was most commonly used in this country. Consequently, merchants needed to keep some in reserve to meet their demands. They placed these stocks in gold with the goldsmiths for safe-keeping. In return for the gold the goldsmiths issued receipts, upon presentation of which the gold would be repaid. From this process two customs naturally emerged. The merchants realised that it was not necessary to go to the goldsmiths and withdraw gold every time they needed money when other merchants who knew or trusted the goldsmith were willing to accept a receipt instead. This was the beginning of the use of paper money. Soon the goldsmiths realised that while people who had deposited gold with them would want to withdraw it at some time, not everyone withdrew simultaneously. Consequently, as long as sufficient gold was retained to meet the demand for withdrawals, the rest could be lent to reliable customers on payment of interest.

From these beginnings gradually emerged the foundations of the modern banking system. Today this is sophisticated, highly organised and efficient, but the basic functions, namely to receive deposits and keep them safe, make loans and facilitate the transfer of money, still remain. In the words of the Radcliffe Report, referring to the London clearing banks:

'The primary business of these banks is the receipt, transfer and encashment of deposits payable on demand . . . individual balances go up and down, depositors come and depositors go, but the total (on deposit) goes on for ever.' (The Report on the Working of the Monetary System [The Radcliffe Report] HMSO 1959.)

The clearing banks

Most of the banking business in England and Wales and a proportion of that in Scotland and Ireland is done by the London clearing banks which are so called because they belong to the Bankers' Clearing House which will be discussed later in this chapter. Until amalgamations took place, these banks were commonly known as the Big Five and Little Six. Mergers have reduced them by almost half, to six, namely, National Westminster, Barclays (includes Martins), Lloyds, National and Commercial, the Bank of Scotland, and Midland.

All these are joint-stock commercial banks. Joint-stock means that they are owned by many people, namely shareholders, and commercial in that they aim to make a profit.

Services provided by banks

One can deposit money with a bank by putting it into either a deposit or current account.

Deposit account. This is a savings account where one puts money with the intention of leaving it for some time. The bank, therefore, has the use of this money and for this reason pays interest on it. It also has the right to demand notice of withdrawal. The amount of interest varies with the length of notice agreed for withdrawal.

Current account. As the name suggests, this type of account is used for day-to-day transactions. Money is constantly going in and out. Consequently, the bank cannot use it as it can money in deposit accounts so no interest is given. Conversely, customers pay bank charges according to the amount they use their accounts and the balance maintained in them.

The distinguishing feature of a current account is a cheque book through which most payments out of the account are made. Cheques are a safe and convenient way of paying bills, save one from carrying large sums of money and supply a record of one's spending. Money can always be withdrawn from one's usual branch of the bank and at other branches by special permission, and up to £50 can be withdrawn from any branch of any of the six clearing banks on production of a banker's card. A statement of account is sent to customers regularly and at other times by request.

A current account may be opened by individuals, firms, associations and other bodies.

To a business a bank offers many valuable services. A current account is necessary for receiving payments made to the firm and making payments owed by it.

Loans and overdrafts.   Facilities for loans and overdrafts are invaluable when a business is short of money. A loan is given on security, for a fixed sum of money and a specific period of time. The borrower pays interest on the sum borrowed for the agreed time.

A firm or individual can also obtain credit from a bank by having an overdraft. Here the bank allows its client to draw cheques for more money than is actually in the account, up to a specified limit. The amount overdrawn will vary from day to day, as money received is paid into the account. Interest is charged on the actual amount overdrawn each day.

Standing orders.   Insurance premiums, hire purchase payments, subscriptions and other regular payments can be paid by standing order. All that is required is to sign a form giving the bank instructions to pay a particular body a certain sum of money on a named date and at a specified branch of a particular bank. Payments will then be made automatically to the payee's account until the instruction is altered or cancelled by the client.

With the introduction of the direct debit system, this service can also be used for varying amounts of money which become due at varying intervals.

These and other credit transfers are paid through the bank giro system, which is also valuable to businesses for the payment of wages and salaries. Bank giro provides a simple means of paying bills. A form showing the name of the payee and the bank and branch where he keeps his account is completed for each account to be paid. One cheque is then made out for the total sum due for all the accounts, thereby saving the cost of individual cheques, stationery and postage for each bill. The bank transmits the amounts named to each of the respective recipients' bank accounts. Many firms encourage their customers to use this method by attaching credit slips to their statements. These forms can also be marked with information useful to their office system.

These credits are cleared in the same way as cheques. The original slips are returned to the bank of origin, which finally sends them back to the firm or individual who has issued them, thereby showing that payment has been received.

Safe custody of valuables.   Important documents and valuables as well as money can be deposited with a bank for safe-keeping.

Many businesses make use of the night safe service, which enables them to put their takings into a bank when it is closed. Cash is placed in a special wallet provided by the bank. It is then dropped through a vent in the wall of the bank and slides into a safe below. This is opened in the morning and the money credited to the appropriate account.

Foreign business. Banks will issue foreign currency and travellers' cheques and arrange to make cash available to the traveller abroad. They will give advice on and assist with obtaining passports.

They also provide valuable information to the businessman about economic conditions and markets abroad, information on foreign clients and full details of import regulations and trade restrictions in other countries. Last, but by no means least, banks will assist firms considerably with, or actually handle, foreign exchange business for them. Useful booklets and progress reports on various overseas markets also assist the exporter.

Other services provided by banks include advice on investments and almost any financial matter, the actual purchase or sale of investments for customers and executor and trustee services.

Each of the joint-stock banks provides booklets giving details of its services free of charge. In addition, the banks publish quarterly and annual reviews which contain articles of general economic and financial interest.

Bank accounting

The assets of every bank must provide liquidity (quick and easy transfer into cash) and profit. There must be sufficient in cash to meet all demands for withdrawals at any one time. There must also be funds to pay staff wages and salaries, overhead and running expenses as well as interest on deposits and dividends to shareholders. The banks achieve these two requirements by carefully planned investment.

Cash reserve

The basis of the British banking system for many years was the established convention of keeping a cash reserve of 8 per cent or cash ratio of 12½–1. Time had proved that if each bank kept this amount of cash in hand and at the Bank of England, there would be sufficient to meet withdrawals. This meant that from every deposit of £100 received by a bank, £8 was kept in cash so that at any given time the cash in every joint-stock bank had to represent at least 8 per cent of its total deposits.

In addition there had to be a liquidity reserve of 20 per cent, making a total liquidity ratio of 28 per cent. It can be seen that in order to do this, banks were able to lend money at varying degrees of liquidity, through the methods described below, to the extent of 11½ times the value of deposits, thereby adding to the flow of money in the economy. Conversely, when large withdrawals were made, thereby reducing their cash reserves, the banks were forced to call in money in order to restore their cash reserves to 8 per cent of their total deposits.

Rates of interest

In 1971 the Bank of England began to introduce new arrangements to control credit and increase competition among the banks. The cartel arrangements whereby all the joint-stock banks had charged the same rates of interest on loans, namely 2 per cent above bank rate, and had paid out deposits at 2 per cent below bank rate, were ended. *Bank rate*, as it had been known, as the cue for the rates of interest charged and received by the banks and indeed, virtually all other financial institutions, was abolished. Its function to act as the minimum rate at which the Bank of England would lend to the discount market, was retained and consequently called the *minimum lending rate*. This meant that the joint-stock banks were no longer tied to the bank rate but were now able to compete with each other and adjust their own interest rates.

The importance of interest rates and the need for them to be flexible enough to reflect more accurately the money supply and demand were recognised in 1981, when the minimum lending rate was removed. The Bank of England no longer states the rate at which it will supply money to the market, but keeps short-term interest rates within an unpublished band. It is able to influence the rate of interest by buying and selling government securities. The rate it charges at any time, therefore, reflects the prevailing money supply and demand. The joint-stock banks set their interest rates in line with this.

Cash and liquidity

The other important change was the abolition of the 8 per cent cash and 28 per cent liquidity ratios. Instead, the banks were required to keep a minimum ratio of 12½ per cent of eligible reserve assets to eligible liabilities. The theory behind control through eligible assets and the effects it produces are little different from the previous cash and liquidity ratios, but it was introduced to make control by the Bank of England more effective by carefully defining the assets it would accept as eligible. These were defined as:

1. cash at the Bank of England;
2. United Kingdom Treasury bills;
3. money at call with the London money market;
4. government bonds with less than one year to run to maturity;
5. local authority bills eligible for rediscount at the Bank of England;
6. commercial bills eligible for rediscount at the Bank of England, up to a maximum of 2 per cent of eligible liabilities.

At the same time, cash and liquidity requirements were also applied to other banks, in addition to the six joint-stock banks, in order to increase the effectiveness of control by the Bank of England over the creation of credit and hence the amount of money in the economy.

The importance of the banks' maintaining various degrees of liquidity is clear. It may be easier to see how they do so by a brief description of some of their assets. Their most liquid reserves, since they are lent out at a low rate of interest and are repayable on demand or at short notice, are:

1. *Money at call and short notice*
   This is money lent mainly to discount houses and bill brokers. That 'on call' is lent overnight and repayable next day, which means that the bank has the right to recall the money but it does so only if it is required. What a discount house has to repay to one bank it can usually borrow from another on the same basis. Money lent at 'short notice' is usually repayable after one or two weeks.

2. *Bills discounted*
   Banks buy bills of exchange and Treasury bills, which have only a short time to run, at less than their face value, then gain the full value on maturity.

Other assets

Investments
Loans to the government, and holdings of securities in banks and other companies, provide a higher return than any of the items mentioned

above but they are not liquid assets. They can be sold to realise cash but this takes time and the price obtained depends on the market value of the securities.

Advances

The least liquid but most profitable of a bank's assets are advances to customers in the form of loans and overdrafts.

Banks, as we saw above, buy Treasury bills and bills of exchange and make a profit when these mature. Bills of exchange have been issued since at least the twelfth century. Today they are used mainly in international trade. A bill of exchange is defined by the Bills of Exchange Act 1882 as: 'an unconditional order in writing addressed by one person to another, signed by the person giving it, requiring the person to whom it is addressed to pay on demand or at a fixed or determinable future time a sum certain in money to, or to the order of, a specified person, or to bearer'. They, therefore, represent cash which will be available in a short time. Government securities held by banks can also be sold to realise cash. Similarly, investments in banks and other companies which have already been mentioned, can be sold. It can easily be seen that, generally speaking, the greater the liquidity, the lower the profit on an investment.

Fig. D

The creation of credit

When a bank agrees to give a loan, it debits the amount in a loan account which it opens in the borrower's name. It then credits the amount in his current account, in other words adding to his credit balance in that account, so that he may then use it to draw cash or cheques as he wishes. The most common method is to use cheques. When these are drawn, the payees present them to joint stock banks. This in turn increases the deposits of the banks and enables them to extend their credit, hence the term 'loans create deposits.'

Cheques

A cheque is a written instruction to a bank to pay to the person or body named on it a certain sum of money. It could be written on anything and, as long as it contained the name of the payee, the amount, date and signature of the person making it, would be valid. However, for convenience banks issue cheques in books.

There are two main types of cheque, namely bearer and order. The first is payable to the bearer of the cheque—the person presenting it at the bank. This is clearly not a very safe way of transmitting money and is not widely used. It does have limited use. For example, a clerk taking a bearer cheque to the bank can immediately obtain money which the firm wants to use as petty cash.

An order cheque instructs the bank to pay the person named on the cheque, or anyone else he wishes to pay. The cheque is therefore a negotiable instrument—it can be passed on from one person to another as a means of payment and be accepted. However, if the payee does pass the cheque to someone else he must first endorse it by signing his name on the back in the same form as it is shown on the front of the cheque. By doing this he makes the cheque payable to the bearer and has, in fact, converted it into a bearer cheque.

Crossings

A crossing on a cheque means that it can only be paid into a bank account.

There are two types of crossing:

1. *General crossing*

   This consists of two parallel lines drawn across the face of the cheque. Sometimes the words '& Co.' are written on the crossing. This is not necessary, but merely a remnant of the past when there were many more banking firms than there are today and most of them were partnerships. People using crossed cheques usually entered the name of the relevant bank on the crossing before '& Co.', thereby making it a special crossing. Payment was then made only to the bank named.

The crossing can be left empty, or '*a/c payee only*' can be written in it, thereby limiting the payment of the cheque to the person named on it. This is a good safety precaution. '*Not negotiable*' can also be inserted as a form of protection. It means that the person receiving such a cheque obtains with it the same title or right to it as the person from whom he takes it. Therefore, if a cheque is lost, found by someone who has no right to it and passed on to a third person who accepts it in good faith, the last party can be asked to make repayment to the rightful owner. The cheque was stolen when it was given to him; therefore, he had no legal claim to it.

It is advisable to use crossed cheques regularly. Books of cheques already crossed are issued by the banks. A person wishing to draw cash from his account or issue an open cheque for some reason merely writes 'pay cash' in the crossing and adds his signature or initials.

2. *Special Crossings*

These comprise two parallel lines drawn across the face of the cheque with the name of a particular bank written between them, e.g.

In fact, the name of the bank written across the cheque without the parallel lines will suffice. The paying bank will then make payment only to the bank named.

Cheque clearing system

One of the main advantages of the cheque system is that a person receiving a cheque can pay it into his bank account, which will be credited with the appropriate amount, even though the cheque has been issued by another bank. For example, Mr X who banks with the Efficient Bank Ltd, writes a cheque for £30 which he gives to Mr Y.

Mr Y presents it to his bankers, Sterling Bank Ltd, who duly credit his account with £30. To rectify the position, the Efficient Bank Ltd, must pay Sterling Bank Ltd £30.

In reality the situation is more complicated than this, of course, since each of the six clearing banks receives cheques from the other five and conversely has had some of its cheques presented to the others in the course of a day.

There are twelve provincial clearing houses situated in the main commercial cities. Each one deals with cheques drawn on and presented to banks within its area.

At the end of every working day each bank sends all the cheques it has received from banks situated outside its own area to its head office. (If there is no provincial clearing house in its area, all the cheques it has received go to head office.) Here all the cheques are sorted into piles according to the banks which have issued them. Totals of the amounts owed by each of the other banks are then compiled. A clerk from each bank takes these to the Bankers' Clearing House where totals are exchanged and balances arrived at. Each bank has an account with the Bank of England. A bank owing money to another writes a cheque for the respective amount, with the effect that its account at the Bank of England is reduced and the balance of the receiving bank's account increased. The whole process is, therefore, completed without the exchange of any cash.

Specialised banks

Merchant banks

Most of the merchant banks which exist today were founded by merchants who had gained a high reputation in their trades and began making short-term loans for international trade. They also enabled traders to obtain credit from other sources because their names became accepted as a guarantee of a person's credit worthiness and security that a bill of exchange drawn by a foreign trader would be paid. This gradually led to their being asked to act as agents for overseas Governments and companies who wanted to obtain quotations on the London Stock Exchange.

Today most of the merchant banks in existence are family concerns and still private companies or partnerships. They all have a long history and still operate from the City of London. The acceptance of credit still forms a very large part of their work. They also advise and assist their clients with mergers and take-overs, provide finance for business projects, particularly those connected with exporting and enable clients to obtain finance elsewhere. In addition, they provide advice on investment to trustees of large funds like friendly societies, pension funds, etc.

The clients of a merchant bank, who are carefully selected, can also obtain all the services of an ordinary joint-stock bank from it. Added to this, they often receive a higher rate of interest on deposits than they would get from one of the clearing banks.

They make credit available in the money market which is the name given to the provision and acceptance of short-term loans as opposed to long-term ones which is called the capital market. The joint stock banks provide most of the finance for the money market. As has been shown already, most of their money at call and short notice is lent in this way.

Discount houses

A very important part of the money market is discounting, since this provides credit. Discount houses specialise in this. Consequently, they can often offer better terms than the banks. They buy bills from traders and banks throughout the world at an agreed price, then re-discount them to banks or the Bank of England, at a higher figure, when the bill is nearer maturity, thereby making a profit. Much of the money used to buy bills is borrowed although the interest paid on it is usually lower than that at which the bills are discounted. Treasury bills are discounted in the same way.

When the discount houses are short of money and cannot borrow it elsewhere, they are forced to turn to the Bank of England which is known as 'lender of last resort'. They have accounts at the Bank. They only borrow from the Bank of England in times of necessity, since they are forced to pay interest at a shorter term lending rate which is usually higher than the rate charged to them by other lenders.

There are twelve main discount houses, all joint-stock companies, which form the London Discount Market Association.

Issuing houses

As the name suggests, these are financial houses which specialise in making or 'floating' new issues of stocks, shares, debentures, etc. for companies, governments and other bodies. Many issuing houses are also merchant banks.

An issuing house will do all the foundation work necessary for the issue of shares. It will check on the financial security and sound control of the company in question, contact a stockbroker to obtain a quotation on the Stock Exchange and complete other formalities. If it is satisfied on these points, it will issue a prospectus. The issuing house will then underwrite the issue or find another body willing to do so—that is, it provides a guarantee to the firm that the capital required will be raised. If the full allocation of shares is not bought when it is offered for sale, the issuing house will buy the balance then sell them on the Stock Exchange when it can. If the issue is over subscribed, the issuing house will allocate the shares. Issuing houses maintain a close interest in their clients' affairs after the issue has been fully completed and offer them advice on financial matters generally. These institutions are engaged in the capital market since they are raising long-term capital.

Changing patterns

During recent years there has been a breakdown of the boundaries between the different types of banks and finance houses as each of them has expanded its activities. Some of this has been achieved by take-overs or mergers with companies operating in a different sphere of the market, or by general development of activities. For instance, the clearing banks now offer medium-term loans to businesses as do the merchant banks and finance houses. Some years ago this service was only provided by the finance house. The same is true of leasing. Generally, there is much more competition among the institutions in the money market which has operated to the advantage of the customer. All the banks have increased their services and attach great importance to marketing. As a result, the clearing banks are much better equipped to advise and assist their customers and businesses in particular.

The changing patterns of competition and the developing roles of the institutions involved are clearly illustrated in the evidence of the Committee of London Clearing Bankers to the Committee to Review the Functioning of Financial Institutions (November 1977).

The Bank of England

The Central Bank, Bankers' Bank, Government's Bank, the Old Lady of Threadneedle Street—all these names refer to one of the oldest banks in existence—the Bank of England.

It was formed in 1694 to make a loan of £1,200,000 to the king who was in urgent need of money for wars. The loan was subject to interest of five per cent per annum.

It is still a chartered company, but was nationalised in 1946 so that all its shares are now held by Treasury nominees. Nationalisation extended its powers over the joint stock banks and formally made it the Central Bank. The bank is controlled by a court comprising the governor, deputy-governor and sixteen directors. All are formally appointed by the Queen.

It is situated in Threadneedle Street near to the Stock Exchange and in the centre of the city of London. In addition there are nine branches of the bank situated in the chief industrial centres of England. They handle work which can be done locally and collaborate with local bank clearing houses.

Why a central bank?

Because finance is of vital importance to the economy as a whole, it is thought unwise and unsatisfactory to leave it all in the hands of private enterprise. As a result, central banks, controlled by the state, have been established in all the developed countries. They operate in the national interest and do not compete in any way with the commercial banks. Since nationalisation no new private accounts have been accepted by the Bank of England, but accounts registered with the bank before 1946 have been retained. Employees of the bank may open private accounts with it, however.

Function

1. *The government's bank*

    The Bank of England provides a banking service for and gives financial advice to the government. The main account is held by the Treasury and is called the Exchequer Account. In addition to this, all government departments have accounts at the bank. All the income the government receives from taxes, fees, loans and other sources is paid into the bank and all payments are made from it.

    The Bank of England also handles income from and payments to other countries and is in charge of the operation of exchange transactions—the conversion of the pound into other currencies. It operates the Exchange Equalisation Account (which was first set up in 1931 when Britain went off the gold standard) to counteract violent changes in the value of sterling on world markets, thereby retaining a level of stability. An important duty of the Bank of

England is to keep in touch with other central banks, be active in the work of the World Bank and negotiate with other international financial institutions. Another important role it plays in the international sphere is that of banker to the Sterling Area.

On the home front, the Bank of England manages the national debt. It acts as the government's agent for the issue and redemption of gilt edged securities. This includes keeping an up-to-date register of stockholders. When the government is short of money it makes temporary loans known as *ways and means advances*.

2. *The bankers' bank*
All the commercial and other banks keep accounts at the Bank of England. Some of their cash reserves are kept in these accounts which can be withdrawn and increased in the same way as individuals use private accounts. It is through these accounts that the cheque clearing system operates as we have already seen.

3. *Rights of note issue*
One of the provisions of the Bank Charter Act of 1844 was that as banks amalgamated they lost the right to issue notes. This gave the Bank of England the gradual monopoly of note issue. It became the only issuer of notes in England and Wales in 1921.

Since 1931, when the gold standard was abandoned, Britain's currency has been a fiduciary one—that is, it is based on trust and backed by government securities, not by gold. The amount of money to be issued is decided by the government and the Bank of England. Coins are then made and issued by the Royal Mint and notes by the Bank of England itself.

4. *Lender of last resort*
This is one of the most important functions of a central bank and it is here that the special lending rate is used. However, this privilege applies only to discount houses which can borrow from the Bank of England when they are short of cash and cannot obtain it elsewhere. The bank does not lend directly to the joint stock banks. When they are in need of funds they can borrow from discount houses which, if they are consequently short of money, can then borrow from the Bank of England.

Control by the Bank of England
The Bank of England exercises control over the joint stock banks and the monetary system, by its influence over the level of bank credit. As we have already seen, one of its chief functions as the government's bank is to act as its agent in carrying out its monetary policy. Control is achieved through the use of four instruments:

1. *Interest rates*
   There is no longer any bank rate or minimum lending rate fixed weekly by the government and the Bank of England. This was abolished in 1981 (see page 101) to allow interest rates more flexibility so that they could more accurately reflect money supply and demand. The Bank of England still has an important function as lender of last resort. However, the rate at which it discounts bills of exchange and that which it charges discount houses for loans when the market is short of money, is no longer a published figure, but varies according to the current supply of and demand for money. The Bank of England charges a rate within an unpublished band, then announces the precise rates it has charged at the end of each day. The bank can, of course, influence interest rates by the buying and selling of government securities as described below.

2. *Open market operations*
   This is the term used when the Bank of England buys or sells government securities in the market, i.e. through the Stock Exchange. The system is used to increase or decrease credit. By selling government securities the bank reduces credit, since members of the public buy them and draw cheques on the joint stock banks to pay for them. The reserves of the banks are, therefore, reduced and in order to restore their 12½ per cent reserve asset ratio, they are forced to reduce their lending. Their first measure to achieve this will be to call in loans to the money market. Discount houses will have to re-discount some of their bills at the Bank of England in order to pay back their loans and will therefore be forced to borrow at the Bank of England's own prevailing lending rate. This tightening of credit will spread beyond the money market.
   Conversely, by buying securities, the bank increases credit. It issues cheques to the sellers, who pay them into their accounts with the commercial banks. They, in turn, present the cheques to the Bank of England for payment, with the result that the amounts are

added to their reserves at the Bank. Each joint-stock bank can, therefore, expand its lending if it wishes to do so. In short, open market operations increase or decrease the amount of money in circulation. Since the abolition of the minimum lending rate, open market operations have become even more important as an instrument of monetary control.

3. *Funding*
When the government needs to borrow money, it does so through the Bank of England. The bank can raise this money by issuing either Treasury bills which are short-term securities or bonds which are long-term. Funding is the term used when the bank issues bonds to finance government borrowing. By doing this, it is adding to the national debt. By varying the proportion of Treasury bills and bonds issued, the government and the Bank of England have an important instrument through which to control the amount of credit available. For instance, if the Bank of England sells bonds and with the revenue buys back Treasury bills from the joint-stock banks, the liquidity of the banks is reduced and they are forced to reduce their lending. The amount of money available in the economy is then also reduced.

4. *Special deposits*
These are deposits which the Bank of England requires the joint-stock banks to keep with it when considered necessary, in addition to its normal cash reserves. This provision was made in 1958. It is used only when considered necessary, and the amount of the deposits varies. The deposits bear interest, but cannot be withdrawn. This scheme provides the bank with another method of reducing the lending powers of the commercial banks.

5. *Direct instructions*
The bank has a further instrument of control. It is empowered by the Bank of England Act 1946 to issue directives to the commercial banks. The same act gave the Treasury power to give direct instructions to the Bank of England. In fact, there has been no need to use these powers by either body since advice or request has been sufficient.

12

INSURANCE

The object of insurance is to guard against the risks of life. It is a form of security which compensates for loss. Its basis is the pooling of risk. A lot of people are prepared to pay out regularly a small sum for a long period, in the knowledge that if a particular contingency occurs they will obtain compensation. In short, the majority pay and the unfortunate few who suffer loss receive compensation from the pool, so that the risk is spread.

The field covered by insurance is almost limitless. It is possible to insure against almost any risk. The amount of the premium will depend upon the likelihood of the risk occurring. To industry and businesses of all types, insurance is essential. Loss of buildings and equipment or serious damage by fire or lightning, for example, would mean that they could not be replaced by many firms if they had to be paid for out of their own funds.

There are four recognised branches of insurance, namely Life, Fire, Marine and Accident, which includes all forms not covered by the previous three classes. In the past, insurance firms used to specialise in one of these areas or have each class of business handled by one particular office. Today, the tendency is to achieve economies and efficiency through larger units. Many amalgamations have taken place among insurance companies and insurance groups have emerged, with the result that all classes of insurance can be obtained with one company or group. There are, however, about forty companies which deal only in life assurance.

The range covered by insurance is as wide and varied as the risks of life. It is a complex and interesting subject. In the short space available here it is only possible to examine it briefly and see the function of insurance and its importance to industry and commerce.

Assurance

It is important to define the term *assurance*. It is used to describe insurance where an agreed sum is paid when a particular event which is bound to happen occurs. Life insurance falls into this category, since the payment of a certain sum by the insurers is guaranteed on the death of the insured. Death is bound to occur. The only uncertainty is when it will happen. The term life insurance is, therefore, incorrect and should be life assurance.

There are two main types of life assurance policy:

1. *Whole Life* where a fixed sum is payable on the death of the insured; and
2. *Endowment* where a stated sum is payable after a number of years or on the death of the insured, whichever occurs first.

Endowment policies represent a form of investment in addition to providing assurance. The minimum for which they can be taken out is usually fifteen years. At the end of this time, the insurance company will pay the insured the total amount he has contributed in premiums, plus profits (in a with-profits policy) which are granted on a percentage basis each year, their amount depending on the prosperity of the company.

Life assurance, therefore, also differs from other classes of insurance in that each policy is a long-term contract with fixed premiums, instead of one which is renewable annually and the rates for which are subject to change from year to year.

Insurance and business
Insurance is invaluable to every business, regardless of its nature or size. Damage to or loss of buildings and equipment by fire, for example, also means the loss of business while repairs are being carried out. All this would bring disaster to a firm if it were not insured against these risks. Compensation paid by the insurance company not only benefits the insured, but also firms who buy from and sell to it, as well as the general public who use its products or benefit from its services. The benefit of insurance is, therefore, not just to the individual or firm immediately concerned but also to the nation.

The risks most commonly insured against by businesses are:

Fire
Fire is an obvious hazard to a firm's property. The standard fire policy also covers damage by lightning and the explosion of gas or domestic boilers. If a fire occurs the insurers will make good the loss incurred, provided that the premium paid covered the full value of the premises

and contents. Some firms obtain only partial cover. In these cases, most policies consequently bear only part of the loss suffered and in the event of a claim the amount of compensation then has to be agreed.

The premium paid for a fire insurance policy will depend on the value of the property insured and the risk involved. Cover against other dangers, such as earthquakes or floods, can be added to fire policies on payment of extra premium.

As mentioned above, a firm may suffer loss of business after a fire, while buildings are being restored and equipment replaced. Trade and profits will suffer as a result. It may take out a *consequential losses* policy to cover this.

Burglary

Insurance against burglary will provide the firm with compensation for loss resulting from goods being stolen and damage to property through an actual break-into the premises, as opposed to simple stealing. As with fire insurance, the amount of the premium will depend on the risk involved. A higher premium will be charged for premises which are not well secured than for those which are well protected.

Fidelity guarantee

Stealing and other dishonest acts by employees, such as embezzlement, are covered by this insurance which can be taken out on a group basis or on individual employees.

Employers' liability

Employers are liable for accidents to employees occurring through their (the employers') negligence and must, therefore, obtain an insurance to protect themselves against this risk.

Bad debts

Firms run the risk that money owed to them by their creditors will not always be paid. They can protect themselves against such losses by taking out a bad debts insurance policy. In exporting, the risk of bad debts is even greater than in the home trade, since sales can be affected by forces outside the control of the importer. The government provides an insurance scheme for exporters to compensate them for sales lost in this way, as a result of currency or market restrictions being imposed by the government of the importing country, or any other political action. This is done through the Export Credits Guarantee Department, which is operated by the Department of Trade and Industry.

Goods in transit
Cover can be obtained for loss of or damage to goods and company property which are being transported from one place to another by rail, road, air or sea.

These are the risks most commonly insured against, but there are obviously others, too, for which firms obtain cover. For example, they are bound to insure, at least for liability to other road users, any vehicles used in their businesses. Finally, there are risks which are non-insurable and those for which the cost of insurance is considered too high. In such cases the business bears the whole risk itself. It is not possible to insure against war risks, for example. While changes in taste, fashion or weather lead to variations in the demand for the products of some firms, they are not likely to insure against them, since the cost would be considered too high.

Principles of insurance
There are four basic principles of insurance. These are the conditions underlying every contract of insurance, whether they are actually written in the policy or not. In some cases, however, amendments to them are made but these are always clearly stated in the policy.

1. *Insurable interest*
   The first essential is that the person wishing to undertake insurance has an interest in the object to be insured. In other words, he must show that he would suffer as a result of its loss or damage to it. This applies equally to life assurance. Without this provision, insurance would be a mere gamble, in just the same way as one gambles when backing a dog or a horse, since one has no claim to the animal, or interest in it, except to obtain a sum of money if it wins.

2. *Utmost good faith*
   This applies to the insurer and insured and requires that all relevant information is given to the insurer and nothing is concealed or misrepresented. Similarly, the insurer must disclose all available facts and information to the insured. Failure to act in good faith

renders the policy void. Consequently concealment of any information by a person taking out insurance entitles the insurer to rescind the contract and, therefore, make no payment in the event of a claim.

3. *Indemnity*

The object of insurance is to enable the insured to recover his loss in the event of a particular hazard occurring, and to be placed as nearly as possible in the same position as he was in before the loss.

The contract of indemnity means that in the event of a claim the insured should recover his loss, but not make a profit. In the case of fire, for example, he will be paid the value of the damaged property and contents at the time of the fire—not the cost price. Similarly, a car insured from new which two years later is involved in a serious accident and consequently written off, will bring compensation from the insurance company to its owner at the market value of the vehicle at the time of the accident.

The principle of indemnity applies to all insurance policies except those for life assurance and personal accident.

There are two connected principles, namely:

4 (a) *Subrogation*

The principle of subrogation gives the insurance company, after it has given the insured full indemnity for his loss according to the terms of the policy, the right to any revenue raised from the sale of damaged goods and the right to claim against any bodies or persons who were in any way responsible for or contributed to the hazard which occurred. Similarly, if a claim is paid by an insurance company following a burglary and the stolen goods are later found, they are then the property of the insurance company.

4 (b) *Contribution*

Sometimes a risk is covered by two or more insurers. The principle of indemnity still applies. In such cases, one insurer pays out the total amount of the loss to restore the insured to his former position financially, and then obtains part of the total from the other insurer(s). In other cases, the amount which can be claimed from each insurer is limited, as in marine policies with Lloyds.

Terms and procedure

A person or body wishing to insure his life or property must first make an application for insurance on a special form giving all relevant details. This is known as the *proposal*. If the insurers accept the risk, the terms and conditions of the insurance on which claims can be made are entered on an official document known as the *policy*. This is, in fact, a contract. Among the details in it will be the amounts which have to be paid and at what intervals. These are called *premiums*.

The insurance market

Most insurance in Britain is provided by mutual societies, joint-stock companies and Lloyd's underwriters. The mutual societies are run almost on a co-operative basis, in that there are no shareholders. The profits are distributed to the policy holders, but they are also responsible for making good any losses which occur. They date back to pre-welfare state days, when groups of people clubbed together to provide a pool from which members could draw in times of sickness and death.

The largest suppliers of insurance are, however, the joint-stock companies, the names of many of which are household words. A few specialise in one section, but most firms handle all risks. Members of the public requiring insurance can contact any of these firms directly. Their funds are invested in British industry and commerce. In fact, more than a third of their total assets are invested in ordinary shares and debentures.

Tariff companies

Companies specialising in the fire or accident branches of insurance fall into two distinct categories—*tariff* and *non-tariff* companies. Tariffs, or rate agreements, have been made by groups of companies, in the light of their collective experience, to ensure that the rates charged for insuring these risks are the most economic, but not too low to meet all possible claims. Policies offered by tariff companies usually cover general risks in each particular class. Extra premiums are charged for cover against any special or additional hazards.

Many well-known insurance companies, and all Lloyd's underwriters, have preferred to remain outside the tariff system so that they are free to fix their own rates.

The tendency now is to move away from the tariff system, while using the rates purely as a guide. Tariffs have been suspended on motor insurance which is the least profitable—or rather, in many cases, the most costly class of insurance—for the insurers. The only tariffs remaining are those for fire which are widely used and thus subject to competitive variation.

Lloyd's

Lloyd's has a long and distinguished history. It is not a company, but an association of insurers known as underwriters, who operate from the same building. Lloyd's began in a coffee house opened by Edward Lloyd in 1689—hence its name. Here merchants, particularly those connected with shipping and other seafaring people, used to meet and transact business. Gradually Lloyd's coffee house became the centre of underwriting business and, for information about shipping, Edward Lloyd periodically published a paper known as *Lloyd's News* which contained marine news. This was the forerunner of the famous *Lloyd's List and Shipping Gazette* which is now published daily.

Lloyd's remains the centre for marine insurance and insures ships from all over the world, but its underwriters also insure other risks.

Lloyd's is run by a committee which must approve a person before he can become a member. Membership comprises over 20,000 underwriting members who are grouped into about 430 syndicates, and brokers who form a link between members of the public and the underwriters.

On becoming a member, every underwriter must deposit considerable securities with the Committee of Lloyd's, which can be used to pay any claims which are made against the syndicate.

In the event of a loss, each member of a syndicate is responsible, to the full extent of his personal possessions, for his share of the liabilities incurred by the syndicate. This regulation and the stringent financial conditions laid down by the committee ensure that those obtaining insurance from Lloyd's underwriters have complete protection. Membership used to be exclusive to men, but since 1969 women who can meet the financial requirements are eligible.

Each syndicate is independent from the rest and is, in fact, in a sense in competition with them. Each one is represented at Lloyd's by an underwriting agent who accepts risks on its behalf.

Insurance is placed with a Lloyd's broker who negotiates with the underwriters on behalf of their clients. The broker is paid commission by the underwriter from the client's premium. Each underwriter states the amount he is willing to underwrite, so that every risk is shared among a number of syndicates and the risks of each syndicate are spread among a number of enterprises.

When an underwriter accepts part of a risk he indicates this by signing his name under the policy, hence the term *underwriter*.

In addition to providing a market for insurance and other services for underwriters, the Corporation of Lloyd's has agents in ports all over the world who transmit information on shipping and assist when ships are in difficulties. Its Register shows particulars of all ships registered in Britain and most foreign ships.

Marine Insurance

This is a very specialised and complex class of insurance. Since it forms such a large and important part of Lloyd's work and is so important to the country, it is discussed briefly below. Insurance of foreign ships is a valuable invisible export.

A marine insurance policy covers the usual hazards of the sea in addition to fire and theft. Ordinary wear and tear, or that caused by rats and vermin, and petty stealing are not included.

The usual types of marine insurance policies are:

1. *Voyage policies* which cover the goods or hull for a specified voyage.
2. *Time policies* giving insurance for a specified period of time not exceeding twelve months.
3. *Mixed policies* covering both a specified voyage and a stated period of time.
4. *Floating or open policies* are used mainly by regular overseas traders to cover all their shipments for a period ahead. The actual period of time will depend upon the shipments and the sum insured. Details of each shipment are then entered on the back of the policy.

Fleet policies can also be taken out to cover several vessels owned by the same person or organisation on one policy. Vessels under construction are usually insured against damage and loss.

Insurance brokers

It has already been seen that in order to obtain any form of insurance from a syndicate(s) at Lloyd's one must first contact a Lloyd's broker. In contrast, one can obtain cover from an insurance company, by approaching it directly. In addition, companies have their own agents who undertake business for the firm on receipt of commission. One can also obtain insurance through a broker. This method has the advantage of obtaining the best terms, since the broker works on behalf of his client and seeks to achieve the best cover at the lowest premium. He is an expert in insurance and has details of the policies offered by all the companies. When a policy is accepted by his client the broker receives commission from the insurance company with which the business has been placed.

13

TRADE, COMMERCIAL AND VOLUNTARY ASSOCIATIONS

Chambers of commerce

Chambers of commerce provide one of the most valuable sources of information and help to businesses of all kinds. They are usually conveniently situated in centres of business throughout the United Kingdom. Their membership is made up of firms from all sections of trade and industry operating in their respective areas. In fact, some chambers, for example, the Birmingham one, are aptly called Chambers of Commerce and Industry. Chambers are associations of businesses and operate to help business in every possible way. Their aim is to further trade.

Each chamber is run independently from the rest, but all collaborate and act collectively to provide information for their members on all aspects of business. Eighty-seven chambers group together to form the Association of British Chambers of Commerce. Some of the British chambers operating abroad are also affiliated to this.

Chambers of commerce are organised on a geographical basis, and exist to serve the needs of their members. It is impossible to list their work specifically, since it varies slightly from one to another. The functions mentioned below give a general picture of the work they do.

Many firms require information and help in exporting. Here chambers of commerce provide valuable contact with other members who have had experience in the area concerned. Information on existing markets, economic conditions, population, customs regulations, trade policy, legal restrictions and other relevant information will be supplied. Members are assisted in appointing agents abroad and introduced to appropriate institutions and government departments at home and abroad. Chambers will assist with the completion of the many relevant documents involved in exporting, and actually issue certificates of origin, certificates of analysis and certificates of weight and quality.

They organise trade missions to other countries and trade exhibitions of all kinds. In short, they assist with all aspects of exporting. A distinguishing feature of chambers of commerce, however, is that they encourage trade both ways and help with imports as well as exports. They receive foreign trade missions visiting Britain and circulate enquiries from traders overseas, to assist their members to import necessary goods or find foreign markets for their products.

Most chambers offer many other services to help members to trade with foreign firms. An invaluable service offered by the twelve largest chambers of commerce is the issue of Export of Commercial Samples carnets to members and non-members. These documents enable a person to export samples to another country temporarily, without having to pay duty or go through any other customs formalities. Further help is provided through the co-operation of the chambers of commerce with the British Export Houses Association which is composed of export merchants, and the Institute of Directors.

On the home front, chambers of commerce provide information on all aspects of legislation affecting industry and trade and advise on economic and trade conditions. They help firms to employ and train staff in salesmanship and export procedures, and provide arbitration services to settle commercial disputes. Commercial education services, language training, interpreter and translator services are provided. The London Chamber of Commerce has a large commercial education scheme which sets commercial examinations at home and abroad.

Most chambers have commercial libraries and many also provide secretarial services.

Lastly, but by no means the least important service they provide, is a meeting place for members. This obviously helps to promote trade, even though its effects cannot be calculated exactly. In addition members can hire rooms in a chamber of commerce building for meetings and other functions, at modest rates.

Chambers of trade

These could be very simply defined as mini-versions of chambers of commerce. Their members are drawn from smaller areas than those of the chamber of commerce and their services, although valuable, are not as wide or far-reaching.

A chamber of trade can be found in most towns. Its members comprise most local traders who represent a wide range of businesses. It is concerned with all matters which may affect trade in the area, from the likely impact of a new road through a town to opening hours for shops, the provision of car parking facilities for shoppers or the effect of proposed legislation on the businesses in the town.

Trade associations

Trade associations are national bodies concerned with a specific trade or part of a trade. Member firms are active in the trade and are drawn from all over the country. These associations exist to provide a single and representative mouthpiece for their members' interests and points of view. In this connection they negotiate with trade unions on matters concerning wages and conditions of work, and make representations to the government and other bodies.

They facilitate the exchange of information among members, keep them up-to-date with movements and changes in the trade and provide other services required by members. For example, a trade association may often give a member firm confidential information about potential foreign agents. Many associations draw up common forms of agreements or contracts to simplify and standardise these procedures. They also regulate trading practices, which may include the regulation of prices, to protect the interests of the trade. To be allowed to operate these must, however, under the provisions of the Restrictive Trade Practices Act 1956, be proved to be in the interests of the public.

Through their membership of a trade association, firms which are in competition against each other co-operate for their mutual benefit.

There is a large number of trade associations in existence. Their size, scope and work vary considerably. Many of them belong to the Confederation of British Industry.

Examples of trade associations are: the Machine Tool Trades Association which comprises manufacturers and importers of machine tools; the Society of Motor Manufacturers and Traders is the main trade association for firms engaged in the motor trade. The Advertising Association draws members from all sections of the industry and includes advertisers, media owners and agencies.

The Confederation of British Industry

Incorporated by Royal Charter in 1965, this is the national representative body of British industry. It is recognised as the main channel for consultation between private industry and the Government. It represents British industry abroad and has permanent offices and staff abroad.

Its membership comprises trade associations, employers' associations and individual firms. Nationalised industries are eligible for associate membership. The Confederation is the central representative body for employers' associations and is, in effect, the employers' trade union, since it represents their views to the government and to the public.

Representatives of the Confederation sit on government advisory committees, other statutory bodies and voluntary bodies concerned with labour matters and other questions affecting industry.

The Confederation provides its members with valuable information and statistics on home and foreign trade. It provides an advisory and consultancy service on all aspects of business, but is particularly helpful with matters relating to exports.

At home the CBI has offices all over the country to give members easy access to its services. It has first-hand information about markets and conditions abroad through the establishment of permanent offices and staff abroad. This also provides direct and constant representation of British industry overseas. Furthermore, it collaborates closely with chambers of commerce on matters of common interest.

Consumer protection

Legislation to protect the consumer against various abuses by manufacturers and traders has existed for more than one hundred years. The recognition of the need for consumer protection, however, is much more recent.

The British Standards Institution was one of the first voluntary bodies to be active in this field. At the end of the Second World War it became involved in standardising the sizes, designs and quality of certain goods, such as nuts and bolts and paint tins, in order to make different makes interchangeable and provide a guarantee to the customer that they could safely do the work for which they were designed. Standardisation also meant that the goods could be produced more cheaply. The work of the BSI has spread far beyond this. It now carries out tests on a wide range of goods. Those which are proved safe and reliable are awarded the BSI kite mark which is a guarantee to the customer that the product has reached a satisfactory standard of safety. The testing of electrical goods is probably its most important contribution in this sphere. (See also page 128.)

In 1957 the Institute's Consumer Advisory Council published *Shopper's Guide*, which was the first comparative testing magazine in Britain. This was one sign of the general awareness that consumers needed information and protection against misleading descriptions, short measure, poor quality and other abuses. It also established a basis for comparing the qualities and prices of similar products. Later, in 1957, a second comparative testing magazine called *Which?*—now widely known and accepted—was published by the Consumers' Association. By 1959, government concern was indicated by the setting up of a committee on Consumer Protection under the chairmanship of J. T. Molony, Q.C. Its recommendations were published in 1962. One result was the formation of the National Consumer Council, in 1963, sponsored by a grant from the government.

By 1963, the work of the Consumer Advisory Council of the BSI had become superfluous as a result of the activities of the government and those of the Consumers' Association. Consequently the Consumer Advisory Council and its publication *Shopper's Guide* disappeared, although the other activities of the BSI were extended and strengthened. This continues to be the case. *Which?* is published regularly and continually increases its field of investigation, thereby making available to the consumer valuable information about goods and services and an independent comparison of them. The Consumers' Association continues to make many valuable contributions in this field. One of these is the provision of information to committees set up by the government from time to time to investigate consumer matters. Many of its recommendations to the Crowther Committee on consumer credit were incorporated into the Consumer Credit Act of 1974.

In 1972, government responsibility for the growing importance of and need for protection of the consumer in the broadest sense, was acknowledged by the appointment of a Minister for Trade and Consumer Affairs. This title soon changed to Secretary of State for Prices and Consumer Protection. In addition, the Fair Trading Act of 1973 created the post of Director of Fair Trading, with responsibility for keeping all consumer affairs under constant review, and power to take action against businesses trading unfairly, breaking the law or failing to keep obligations to customers. The creation of these two departments revealed the government's commitment to the consumer, and this commitment has been continued by successive governments, although inevitably with some changes. Currently, the Secretary of State for Trade and Industry has the responsibility for competition policy and consumer affairs, these duties being assigned to two specific Divisions within the Department. Closely linked to this, is the encouragement of fair trading, which is the responsibility of The Office of Fair Trading, an independent government agency led by the Director General of Fair Trading.

To sum up, consumer protection now is provided by these three main groups:

1. The government;
2. Voluntary independent bodies;
3. Local authorities.

1. *The government*

The most important source of protection is, of course, legislation. This covers a wide range of goods and possible areas of abuse. The Consumer Protection Acts, 1961 and 1971, give the government broad powers to enforce measures to ensure the safety of all goods. Other legislation is more specific. The Weights and Measures Acts, which were revised by the Act of 1963, ensure that quantities are uniform and clearly marked on goods and make the sale of short weights and measures illegal. Inspectors ensure that these provisions are complied with. The Trade Description Acts, 1968 and 1977, require clear and accurate descriptions of goods offered for sale. The Prices Act, 1974, requires prices or unit prices to be marked on goods offered for sale. Standards of quality and hygiene for food are ensured through the Food and Drugs Acts. The abolition of resale price maintenance in 1964 enabled retailers to sell their products at prices they considered suitable, rather than those enforced by the manufacturer which were, in many cases, sufficient to keep the less efficient traders in business. The general result of this, though hard on the small shopkeeper, has been lower prices to the consumer. Legislation on restrictive practices and monopolies is also based on consideration of the interests of the public. The Consumer Credit Act passed in 1974 is far-reaching and replaces all previous legislation on consumer credit (including hire-purchase).

Government responsibility in this sphere is also exercised through its departments. The Department of Trade and Industry, for instance, has an overall concern and authority in those two fields. Any questions of consumer interest or concern can, therefore, be raised with the Secretary of State in the House of Commons. The Department of Trade and Industry is also responsible for ensuring that certain legislation relating to the consumer is correctly administered. For example, it sees that the Weights and Measures Laws are being followed throughout the country. The Department of Health ensures that the provisions of the Food and Drugs Act are being met, and provides new standards and legislation when necessary.

Each of the nationalised industries has a special committee which investigates consumers' complaints and enquiries. Questions can also be raised through Members of Parliament to the ministers concerned, in the House of Commons. Most of the marketing boards also have consumer committees.

The Council of Industrial Design, which was set up by the Government and sponsored by a grant from the Department of Trade and Industry, plays its part by promoting higher standards of design for all types of goods. A selection of designs it has praised particularly are displayed at the Design Centre in London. A register of approved designs is kept and awards are given annually for selected well-designed goods.

2. Voluntary and independent bodies
Some of the work of the British Standards Institution and the Consumers' Association, which are probably the two most important bodies in this category, has already been mentioned. It is useful, however, to look briefly at their organisations.

British Standards Institution.   This is a voluntary, non-profit-making body which was formed by Royal Charter. It is run by a council, whose membership is made up of representatives from employers' and workers' associations, government departments and professional bodies. The standards it sets are voluntarily accepted by manufacturers and consumers. (Standards for a few specific goods, for example, paraffin heaters and motor cycle safety helmets are legally enforceable.) They are drafted by committees of manufacturers, distributors, technical experts and in some cases consumers. Goods which conform to these standards are allowed to bear the famous 'kite mark'.

Consumers' Association.   This is a non-profit making company. Its revenue is raised from members' subscriptions and the sale of its publications. It is organised by a council elected from among its ordinary members. The number of ordinary members is limited and comprises people who have been invited because of their interest in consumer affairs. None of the council is paid and because of the need for impartiality when testing and comparing goods, members may not be employed in industry, commerce or advertising. This is one of the main reasons for the public's trust in the Association and its consequent popularity and success.

Actual testing of the goods is done by outside specialist organisations such as university departments. The Association provides a grant for its Research Institute, which carries out research on goods and services and publishes reports.

In addition to *Which?*, the Association publishes the *Good Food Guide* and the *Drug and Therapeutics Bulletin*.

Other bodies.   The Good Housekeeping Institute awards its own mark and name to manufactured articles it considers reliable, safe and of good quality.

There are also television programmes in which goods and services are analysed, criticised and compared. Independent television has a strict code with which all its advertisements have to comply and all are examined by a committee before they are allowed to appear before the public. For the general field of advertising the Advertising Association has established the Advertising Standards Authority as an independent body, to promote and preserve high standards of advertising.

There are many other bodies giving protection for the consumer. The AA and RAC for example, issue a guide to the standard of food and accommodation in hotels and in so doing help to improve their quality. They also examine garage services and represent the motorist generally.

Local independent consumer groups have been set up all over the country and collectively form the National Federation of Consumer Groups.

3. *Local authorities*

Local government authorities support central government action on consumer protection as in other aspects of work. They also implement legislation or ensure that its provisions are carried out. Local government is responsible for appointing inspectors to ensure that the Weights and Measures Acts are being followed by shops and other specified places in their areas. They aid the consumer in any other ways that seem desirable in their particular areas. Citizens' Advice Bureaux provide an advisory service and answer individual consumers' problems.

14

CONSULTANCY AND OTHER SERVICES

In order to operate efficiently, the firm depends on many other services in addition to those mentioned in previous chapters. As industry and its methods advance, specialisation increases and firms become more dependent on each other.

Advertising

Most businesses trade in highly competitive and increasingly specialised markets. To maintain or increase their sales they must keep their products in the public eye and ensure that consumers are constantly reminded of their existence. It should be remembered that, for most products, advertising increases the total amount sold by *all* producers in the market by relatively little. The main outcome of effective advertising is to increase or maintain the *share* of the market held by the product being advertised. In other words, the sales of one product are being increased at the cost of other brands.

While advertising, therefore, increases competition between firms, there is also constantly increasing competition within the field of advertising itself.

Something in the region of £3,000 million is spent annually on advertising in Britain (1.3 per cent of gross national product).

The medium which accounts for the largest part of this is press advertising. The next largest sum is taken by television advertising. The other main media are posters, outdoor signs, films and radio.

Advertising has two main functions. The first is to *inform* the public of the existence of goods. The second is to *persuade* people to buy them. Without advertising, consumers would probably not be aware of all the goods on the market. Through it, they can be told what is available in a particular market, the nature and qualities of the products, their price and where they can be obtained. In order to increase their sales, firms try to show how their products differ from those of their competitors and so persuade people to buy them. For the most part, the persuasive part of advertisements makes them more interesting than if they were purely factual.

Some advertising is solely informative. That in technical journals, for example, merely informs its readers of the qualities of a product. Most advertising aimed at the general public, however, contains an element of information and persuasion. Constant repetition is a form of persuasion. It has been proved that the public needs to be reminded of the existence of even well-known brands of goods if their sales are to be maintained. As competition increases, so must advertising.

Not only do firms within the same market compete against each other, but there is also strong competition between markets. As has been seen in a previous chapter, the gas boards, although they have the monopoly of the gas industry in their areas, are competing against the electricity boards which also have a monopoly.

There are secondary functions of advertising. Certain products we buy and services we receive are subsidised by it. The price we pay for a newspaper or magazine, for example, is only a fraction of its actual cost. The balance is obtained in revenue from advertising. Similarly, commercial television is paid for by the commercials which appear on it.

Since advertising increases sales it also leads to the use of mass production methods and other large-scale economies which make the product cheaper for the consumer, or at least prevent the price from rising. It can further be argued that, in order to maintain the increased sales resulting from advertising, firms need to keep their products at a high standard. The result is that the consumer also benefits from higher quality.

Economists argue that advertising is also necessary to maintain full employment, since a reduction in advertising would result in a fall in sales, which would eventually lead to a reduction in the amount of labour required and so to unemployment.

Finally, it should be remembered that advertising constitutes an industry in itself and employs a large number of people directly and indirectly. Industry and the consumer in Britain, and most other highly developed countries, depend on advertising.

Advertising agencies
Because advertising is so competitive and specialised, all campaigns are highly planned and geared to a particular market. Time of presentation, method, approach and media to be used, and many other factors are all carefully considered and calculated. Most firms employ an advertising agency to do this work for them, since it is staffed by specialists

in advertising. An agency usually receives a fee from the firm whose products are being advertised and a commission from the media owners.

Apart from the expertise and technical know-how which an agency can offer to the firm whose goods are being advertised, agencies also benefit the media owners, who would otherwise have to deal with a large number of individual advertisers instead of a few agencies.

For any firm, an advertising sales campaign is successful only if the profit from the resulting increase in sales is greater than the cost of the campaign.

Public relations departments of firms make an important indirect contribution to advertising, since they are concerned with preserving and promoting the good image of their firms.

Standards and control

The Advertising Association is the trade association for the whole industry. Its membership comprises agencies, advertisers, owners of advertising media and others concerned with advertising. In 1962 it set up the Advertising Standards Authority, an independent body, with the object of promoting and enforcing the highest standards of advertising. It does this particularly through the British Code of Advertising Practice.

The Advertising Inquiry Council is also an independent body which aims to represent the interests of the general public in scrutinising advertisements and trends in advertising.

The agencies' representative organisation is the Institute of Practitioners in Advertising.

Advertisements are subject to the provisions of the Trade Descriptions Act 1968. In addition to this and the general controls imposed by the bodies mentioned above, specific requirements and codes are laid down by the media owners. The Television Act gives the Independent Television Authority the duty and power to exclude from television any misleading advertisements. Every advertisement is carefully and critically examined before it is allowed to appear on television. Its stringent code of advertising standards is prepared by ITV's Advertising Advisory Committee which also examines the advertisements submitted for showing on television.

Market research

Research is an important forerunner of any sales campaign. For a firm's products to sell successfully it is essential to know the type of people they are designed for and the qualities and features they will require in the goods. A product must appeal in order to sell. The wrong appeal is a mistake which companies cannot afford.

To ensure that its product has the right appeal, a firm must investigate potential markets. It will first examine and assess its own past records by product, area, sales technique, etc. Public opinion is then sought by conducting consumer surveys. Surveys usually take the form of questionnaires, or perhaps in the first instance trial samples which are then followed by questionnaires. These are given to a cross-section of the potential consumer market for the product in question, to assess reactions to it. Surveys and samples must be well conducted by experts in order to be useful and produce valid answers.

The firm will then examine the product itself and all its characteristics including name, appearance, contents, price and packaging. The results of this investigation are then compared with the findings of the consumer survey. Most large firms have their own market research departments. Advertising agencies also undertake this work and many companies elect to delegate it to them.

Market research is usually conducted before an advertising campaign is launched to determine that the best medium is used, in terms of the number of people it can reach and the effectiveness of advertising in it compared with other media.

Advice and help on exporting

This is another sphere in which the firm obtains specialist help and advice from many organisations outside the company.

The first essential is to ensure that the policies which the potential exporter is following give him the best chance of exporting successfully. Some manufacturers are better employed concentrating on making their products more competitive with imports being sold in their home market.

There are three main stages in exporting on which a firm needs advice and help. These are:

1. Marketing overseas—assessing the market, the type of product required, potential demand, existing competition, restrictions and any legal requirements, etc.;

2. Export and shipping documentation procedures and provision of finance for the venture;
3. Providing credit for overseas buyers.

1. *Marketing overseas*

Help with marketing can be obtained from chambers of commerce, trade associations, the Confederation of British Industry, the Institute of Export and the joint stock banks. Merchant banks and export houses will also assist with marketing as well as with the other two stages mentioned above. Export houses generally cover all activities involved in exporting. They will provide manufacturers' agents, export managers and factors to act for the exporter. Lastly, the government provides very valuable assistance to exporters through the Department of Trade and Industry. This includes information services (which are continually being expanded), advice and practical help. It will pay part of the expenses of firms taking part in trade fairs and missions organised through the British Overseas Trade Board. From the embassies and consulates abroad, it obtains samples of goods manufactured overseas to enable the potential exporter to see at first-hand and examine the goods it is going to compete against. The department provides assistance in commercial disputes with overseas buyers. Not least among the information services offered by the department is the *Export Service Bulletin*, which is issued three times a week and gives general information about trading conditions abroad, as well as details of overseas contracts for which tenders are invited. *British Business* is also a valuable publication which gives up-to-date information on markets abroad and opportunities for export. These are only a selection of the services offered by the department to exporters.

2. *Export and shipping documentation and finance*

For advice and help in such matters as shipping documentation and other export procedures, the exporter should contact a chamber of commerce, chamber of trade, merchant bank or export house. The same bodies will advise on how to obtain finance for the venture, but generally more specific help can be obtained in this sphere from merchant banks, joint-stock banks or an export finance house.

There is a large measure of co-operation between all the organisations offering help to the exporter. Most of them are able to assist with all aspects and stages of an export venture but where they cannot give positive assistance they can put the exporter in touch with an organisation which offers specific help.

The effect of major government policy on export projects cannot be overestimated, since it sets the framework within which the exporter works and affects the profitability of selling products abroad. Tax incentives, such as the export rebate scheme and assistance for financing exports, do much to encourage firms to sell their goods overseas and make the task much easier for them. Tariff policies, trade agreements and general company taxation can also do much to assist the exporter, as they have in recent years during the British export drive. On the other hand they can operate in a negative way or actually discourage firms from exporting.

3. *Providing credit*
Finally, on the question of providing credit for overseas buyers, exporters can obtain help from the organisations already mentioned, but in particular from merchant banks, export houses and, sometimes, joint-stock banks.

The Export Credits Guarantee Department
Having completed the three stages of exporting, the exporter runs various risks. An order may be cancelled after it has been dispatched or while it is being completed to specific requirements, or goods which have actually been sent may not be paid for. The imposition of currency or import restrictions by the government of the country to which the goods are being imported, the outbreak of war, fighting or disorder and many other circumstances outside the control of the importer can cause considerable financial loss to the exporter. It was to offer protection against such risks that the Government set up the Export Credits Guarantee Department under the auspices of the Department of Trade and Industry. As its services are so important it is worthy of special mention.

The ECGD provides insurance against the buyer's failure or inability to pay for the goods six months after the accepted date on which they were due. An exporter who has taken out a policy with the ECGD and suffers this hazard will receive 85 per cent of the value of his loss. The other main risk covered by this department is cancellation of an order after shipment has been made. In the event of a claim, the exporter must bear the first 20 per cent of the loss (i.e. of the full price of the goods) and the ECGD will pay 85 per cent of the remainder. If the contract is with a foreign government this is extended to cover cancellation while the goods are being produced. Compensation paid by the ECGD is 90 per cent of the loss sustained. In addition, the department will arrange finance for exporters at fixed rates of interest and, in some cases, loans can be made to overseas buyers of capital goods so that the exporter can be paid in cash. A recent addition is some protection against high and unforeseen rises in costs of large exports of capital goods.

In addition to these insurance facilities, the ECGD guarantees complete repayment to banks providing finance to exporters who are insured. By this means, the government helps exporters to obtain loans and enables the banks to provide the finance at favourable rates of interest, which also helps the exporting firm.

Conclusion

As technology advances and specialisation increases, firms will become more dependent on each other. The extent to which each organisation uses the services of outside agencies and bodies is likely to increase. The office already uses management consultancy services, staff agencies, computer and printing services and many others and the trend will certainly continue.

PART II

THE ORGANISATION
AT WORK

15 ━━━━━━━━━━━━━━━━━━━━━━━━━━━━━━━━

ORGANISATION THEORY

Business activity of every kind requires organisation to ensure successful progress. A generally accepted understanding of 'organisation' is the combination of planning, and defining of, delegation responsibilities in each of the various management functions, with the consequential relationships carefully set out and agreed.

The theory of organisation assumes that management will use the various methods of organisation, namely 'line', 'functional', 'line and staff', where appropriate with the aim of establishing the most suitable method for the particular circumstances of the business.

There can be no set pattern or rule. Any one or a combination of all the customary types of organisation patterns may be used. They are summarised in the following pages.

Line organisation

This would be appropriate for a business operated within very clear separate departments, with the person in charge of each department having complete authority—subordinates in each department being responsible only to one superior. Each departmental head would thus have the same standing and in general equal remuneration, none having specific authority over another.

This is illustrated in the chart (Fig. 1) on the next page.

The relevant disadvantages and benefits of line organisation can be summarised simply as follows:

Disadvantages

Communication between departments is not made easy as everything must, presumably, pass through the respective departmental heads, and thus a degree of 'red tape' arises.

Benefits

There is a clear definition of responsibilities and precise duties which, of course, is absolutely essential to maintain efficiency with control and, consequently, discipline is easier to maintain.

Fig. 1

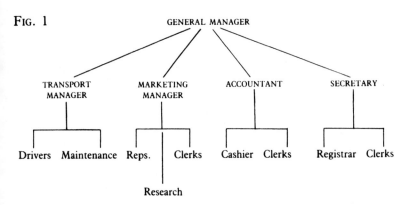

N.B. *A simple exposition of line organisation, which in practice would be more detailed.*

Functional organisation

In normal conditions only small firms with limited activity would use line organisation, and the alternative of functional organisation is preferable in larger concerns requiring a greater degree of flexibility. The principle of this type of organisation is that functional or specialist work which is common to every department must be in the hands of such specialists who carry out that function or work for *all* departments. A simple example of this is the central typing pool.

A functional organisation chart could be prepared on the lines of Figure 2 overleaf.

The relevant advantages and benefits of this type of organisation can be summarised in simple terms as follows:

Disadvantages
A danger to discipline because instructions from different sources could conflict unintentionally.

Benefits
The 'specialists' become experts and are able to pass on their knowledge and experience to subordinates and colleagues.

Fig. 2

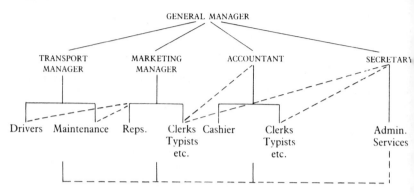

N.B. *A simple exposition of functional organisation—in practice would be more detailed.*

Line and staff organisation

Some companies, recognising the respective benefits of both line and functional organisation, operate these under the 'line and staff' system.

Whatever system is used, there is a fundamental necessity for all concerned to realise that the principal purposes of organisation charts are to establish lines of authority, responsibility, delegation and communications.

Delegation

In the efficient operation of any kind of business activity, delegation must be the essential factor in good management. It must, however, always be a two-way traffic system. Whilst it is good and sound practice to delegate responsibility down or along the line, there must always remain the necessity of reporting up or back to the authority which delegated. In this way ultimate authority and responsibility are preserved. To delegate only without providing for any reporting back is the worst possible kind of management and could be described as foolhardy in the extreme.

The authority delegating must also ensure that the work being delegated is well within the capacity and ability of those to whom it is delegated.

Communications

All the foregoing leads, logically, to a brief mention of essential features of good communications. Delegation involves communication of the two-way kind described, and it is, therefore, obvious that the first requirement in any form of communication is that it should be understandable to all concerned.

This study is not concerned with modern methods of electronics or telecommunications. It is emphasised, however, that whatever method is used, however modern, communication is completely useless and wasted unless it is clearly understood on receipt.

A useful criterion in communicating within a business concern is to consider, *who, what* and *how*—*Who* must receive the message? *What* must the message contain? *How* must the message be sent or given?

Clear decisions on each of these three must be a main factor in good communications.

When deciding how the message must be sent, it should be noted that not only the written or typewritten word or messages by telephone or telex are involved. There is often great value in conveying a message by means of a meeting, whether formal or informal. There is a great advantage in an informal meeting when the two-way communication can operate fully in a free discussion with all concerned.

16 ―――――――――――――――――――――――――

COMMITTEE SYSTEM

Purpose of committees

The purpose of the committee system will be clearly understood by first considering a definition. The dictionary definition of the word 'committee' is:

'one or more persons to whom some special business is committed by a court or assembly or other body of men'.

This definition fits the needs of the business world in which committees are being used to a growing degree, but we should examine the committee system from the legal and practical angles.

In every sphere where men and women assemble for any kind of activity, there are occasions on which it is necessary to refer—or *commit*—some matter for detailed consideration. Examples which spring readily to mind are:

Parliament

Proposed legislation contained in a Bill before the House is referred to a committee for detailed examination—hence the term 'Committee stage on the Bill'.

Local government

A County Council, Town Council, or District Council appoints committees to deal with the work of specific departments.

Associations and societies

The Annual General Meeting elects a Committee of Management and sub-committees for special matters.

Commerce

The shareholders elect directors who in turn appoint works, staff, welfare, production and other committees.

The foregoing is only a brief list to illustrate in outline the purpose of a committee, but it is important to emphasise the fundamental principle, namely:

The appointing body must expect to receive a report back from the committee.

Those to whom business or responsibility is committed must report back to their appointers or electors.

The appointing body may be too large to meet and act collectively, or there may be factors demanding close attention to detail. All or any of these circumstances result in the setting up of a committee, operating within principles which are equally applicable to the public or private sectors.

Characteristics of committees

In the setting up of any committee clear decisions must be taken on two important points, as described below:

1. *Terms of reference*

It is important and desirable for all concerned to know in advance the precise scope of work to be handled by the committee, e.g. the limits of its authority, the nature and scope of the report, the frequency of reports, and the persons or authority to whom such reports are to be made.

All this detail must be set out clearly by those appointing the committee, and the detail is known as 'terms of reference'.

2. *Composition*

The decision to appoint the committee will include the number of seats or number of persons to serve. The actual individuals may also be named in the resolution of appointing, and provision may be made for the members of the committee to co-opt or add others to serve, within the maximum number prescribed for the committee.

Normally those appointing the committee will also appoint the chairman and secretary, to ensure the adequate operation of the committee.

Classification

Committees can, in general, be classified under the following main headings:

1. *Executive*

Usually appointed by associations, clubs or societies, with terms of reference giving powers of management and financial control, reporting back to the Annual General Meeting.

Commercial concerns, i.e. limited companies, banks, insurance companies, etc. appoint boards of directors who operate entirely within the committee system, reporting back to the shareholders assembled at the Annual General Meeting, or if necessary at a Special or Extraordinary General Meeting.

2. *Statutory*
Local authorities are required by law to appoint 'statutory committees' for such departments as Health, Finance, Education, Housing, etc., all reporting back to the regular meetings of the Council.

3. *Standing*
A committee appointed for a single item as set out in the terms of reference would be a standing committee, and would be dissolved on submission of its report. It has only limited power.

The best example of this is in the House of Commons when a standing committee is appointed to consider a Bill.

Another example is a committee of inquiry which also has a similar function to report back on a 'once for all' basis.

4. *Ad hoc*
This is a term used referring to a small committée set up for a special short-term purpose, perhaps to organise a special event, but the principle of reporting back must also apply.

Advantages
The principal advantage of the committee system lies in the fact that committees are able to give close and careful consideration to the matters 'committed'. The proceedings of meetings are not usually restricted by compliance with the recognised 'rules of debate'. There is thus a free exchange of opinion and ideas which allows every aspect of the matter under discussion to be examined. The exchange of ideas usually has a positive result.

Disadvantages
Postponement of decisions is regarded as one of the main disadvantages of the committee system, because the appointment of a committee inevitably means delays. There is often an unavoidable time lag in calling the committee members together for a mutually convenient date. More than one meeting will probably be necessary to enable an

agreed decision to be reached. This applies particularly to standing committees.

Some committees suffer from inadequate chairmanship resulting in compromise or weak decisions, or indefinite action, and this leads inevitably to further delay.

Some committees also assume, quite improperly, powers not contained in their terms of reference. They either go far beyond what is appropriate or, in some cases, withhold relevant information from the report when it is submitted.

Procedure

Following the creation of a committee with adequate terms of reference, and its composition decided, the secretary finds the most convenient date and place for the majority to attend the first meeting.

He must issue a clear notice of date, time and place, accompanied by the agenda, whose content should be agreed beforehand with the committee chairman.

Adequate chairmanship of the meetings is a prime factor in the success of a committee's work. It must be remembered by the chairman that the main purpose of the committee is to have a full interchange of free opinion, while he must not let the meeting drift away from the point under discussion. The chairman must allow discussion to be as full and relevant as possible, and so ensure that the purpose for which the committee was appointed is achieved.

Minutes of the proceedings must always be compiled, usually by the secretary. These will contain only the decisions or findings on which the committee will report to the appointing body. In the case of statutory committees of a local authority, the minutes comprise the report to the ensuing council meeting, with recommendations of action for adoption or rejection.

Subject always to good procedure at meetings, and especially to good chairmanship, modern committee procedure will always play a valuable part in the success of any portion of the public or private sector when issues are to be settled in a truly democratic manner.

17

INTERNAL ORGANISATION AND CONTROL OF BUSINESS

As a logical first step in considering internal organisation and control of business of any size, the various component sections or groups of people who are (or become) involved in the activities of a business company should be understood.

The prime aim of any business company is to make a profit, to be used by the directors in further development and reward those who have invested capital in the company.

To achieve this aim, however, the directors must have the participation of the various groups who themselves contribute outside and inside the business. Whilst this contribution of effort and purpose leads to the success of the business, the groups may well have their own reasons or motives irrespective of the business.

This important principle is illustrated here in Fig. 3.

Fig. 3

GROUP PARTICIPATION IN BUSINESS

Group	Action	Aim
A. Shareholders	Purchase of shares	Dividends and capital gain
B. Debenture holders	Purchase of debentures	Interest on investment Possible profit on sales of debentures
C. Senior executives	Professional skill or knowledge	Salary, and progression Progressive career Security
D. Other employees	Effort and skill	Wages Security
E. Suppliers	Equipment, or materials, or services	Profit Continued business connection

(*continued*)

F. Customers, or clients	Payment	Satisfactory goods or services
G. Directors	General control of all Departments. i.e. 'direction' by Directors	Company growth (and personal gain on own shareholding)

The foregoing is a simple exposition of an economic principle, but is set out to show that the ultimate necessity in any business is the final control of the directors to ensure fullest participation from all component groups.

This study is concerned only, at this stage, with the control factor and it will be helpful to the student to consider the range of such control throughout the usual departments of a normal manufacturing concern. This range is summarised below in a logical sequence.

Finance
Capital raised by shares or debentures.

Planning
Research or projects
Tests of materials and processes
Market research
Designing of models, packaging, sizes, etc.

Purchasing
Supply of best materials at economic price and at required time.
Stock control.

Marketing
A complex and essential function which is described in chapter 20.

Manufacture
Producing the finished goods in the required range of sizes, packets, etc. at the required time.

Personnel
Assembly of adequate numbers of staff and workpeople to operate fully every department. The filling of vacancies, training schemes

and liaison with appropriate industrial training boards, welfare schemes, canteen facilities.

Secretarial services
All administrative and clerical arrangements. Legal requirements and liaison with appropriate government departments, directors' meetings and committees.

Registrar
The maintenance of shareholders' and debenture holders' register and compliance with company law. Payment of dividends and interest to shareholders and debenture holders respectively.

Accounting
Maintenance of all accounting books and records, production of financial results each half year, receipts and payments, salaries, wages, banking.

The extent of control over all these departments at director, executive and supervisory level must always be such as to ensure that each department is able to play a full part in the success of the whole enterprise. The strength of any chain is that of its weakest link—thus the strength of the enterprise is the strength of the weakest part.

As with the chain, so with the business and any weakness must, accordingly, receive prompt and effective attention to ensure the continued strength and progress of the remainder.

Control, therefore, is a fundamental necessity in the success of any business.

18

DEPARTMENTS IN THE ORGANISATION I

General administration
An organisation of any size must divide its activity in order to specialise and ensure responsibility for various aspects of work. Even a small firm containing two partners will tend to divide in this way, through one partner concentrating upon the production or internal side of the business and the other occupying himself with selling the product and external relations.

Figure 4 shows a chart of an imaginary company, starting with the shareholders, who are the owners and who elect from among themselves a chairman and board of directors. One of the directors will become the managing director, who is the chief executive of the company. That is to say, he takes command of the daily running of the organisation, interprets the policy decided by the board of directors and translates it into practical effect. In theory he is just a director like the others when he is in the board room and has only one vote, but in practice he is a very powerful voice and carries great weight. Sometimes working directors are appointed to the board, the accountant or the marketing man, for instance. These are theoretically equal to the managing director in the boardroom, but, of course, are subordinate to him in their daily work. The company secretary is a legal requirement for a company and he attends the board meetings too.

Figure 4 does not attempt to distinguish between line and function, except to indicate that there is a very strong line element in production and marketing, for obviously in the areas of marketing and selling a product, there is a very distinct necessity for authoritarian instruction to complete specific tasks.

Production
According to Adam Smith, the true end of production is consumption, by which he implies that goods and commodities which are unsaleable or produced in excess are not only useless, but are wasteful of national and human resources. This will apply not only to a company's operations, but also to the reasons for its formation.

FIG. 4

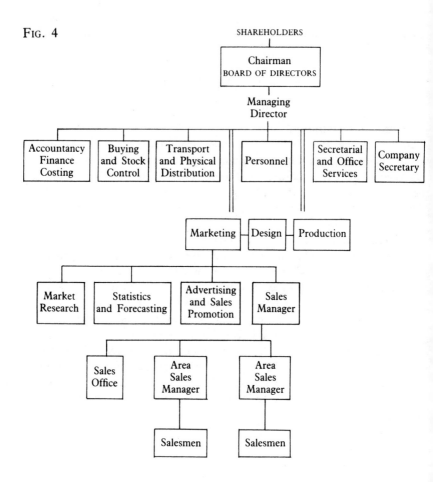

Production planning bases

The broad determinants of the nature and volume of what will be provided, and how it will be planned in detail, rest on:

1. Corporate plans, company style, profit intentions, general policy.
2. The company's capability or size, skills and financial capacity.
3. The market, and the company's own marketing skills to secure the volume and profitability desired.
4. More specifically, the sales forecast, a realistic statement of what to make, how much, when and at what price.

The methods of production

These vary with the nature of the product or service. The printing of a daily newspaper differs from that of a wedding invitation, and both are quite unlike a limited issue of an art work. Volume, demand, quality and keeping qualities are all important.

The three main categories of production are generally recognised as: one-off (or job), batch, and flow line, and are described below.

One-off. This is usually employed for custom-built, individual projects to meet specific needs. A ship, steelwork for a bridge, the engines for an aircraft carrier are examples. As the name implies, the plans and craftmanship are directed to a single product (a Savile Row tailor works this way, too) and the speciality of such production is expensive.

Batch production. A manufacturer may make many products—for example, hammers, pliers, screwdrivers and spanners; or he may make wheels of various shapes and sizes. These could be made in batches of 500, 1,000, 10,000 or 100,000 of each article.

It requires planning to ensure that the right labour and machines are available, and the correct components and raw materials are assembled all at the appropriate time. Batches can be made manually, but the benefit comes with the use of mass-production methods of standardisation of parts and runs on high-speed repetitive machines. Batch sizes will vary, and some will be made for stock as well as for special purposes.

Flow line. This system usually needs heavy investment in the equipment and the availability of raw material supplies. it requires an assured market to ensure the steady flow of goods away from the factory. It demands detailed and high-quality planning, great confidence in the market support and is very sensitive to seasonal fluctuations. Stopping and starting are expensive, and also the high cost of plant makes idleness very expensive. Uninterrupted flow of materials and activity is the secret of high-volume and low unit-cost production, but it is less flexible than batch production and new products must be very carefully planned. Flow line is used for cement, steel-making, canned goods, bulk chemicals and some processes never stop, continuing day and night. Flow line processes are frequently automated, because the rhythmic repetition of activities lends itself to mechanical substitution.

Planning

The sales forecast is not a document solely for the marketing department; other departments also contribute to and use the final draft. Research, development and design are concerned with new products, the accounts department must consider financial provision, assessing the best use of capital, and the production department suggests how to ensure a good product. More than this, the sales forecast is the blueprint for planning in all departments—and none more so than in the production department, which will set its objectives for:

1. Quality
2. Volume and timing (how much and when)
3. Costings and budget
4. Provision of new manpower, machinery and accommodation.

A programme must then be set, showing:

1. Supply and timing of raw materials, tools, and operational supplies—fuel, lubricants, etc.
2. Exact timetables of machine availability
3. Plans for extra buildings and installation of new machines
4. Labour, i.e., skills review, recruitment, redundancy or training.

From this programme, operational schedules will be issued to production units. These will specify in detail the processes to be completed, with timings, raw material and labour usage, right down to the removal, storage and recording of finished goods.

Such planning requires high-quality office skills, critical path and network analyses, detailed schedules supported by progress charts, requisitions for stores and instructions for materials handling. The planning will set out the objectives for all, so that standards are laid down for quality, quantity, timing, costs and so forth. Management consists not only of planning, but also control—the observance and maintenance of the set standards.

For this, good statistical communication must be established, bringing relevant detail to management for approval or remedial action. Further, to ensure sustained efficiency and economy there must be monitoring sections, such as:

1. Quality control   to maintain standards of products
2. Budgetary control   to watch all costs
3. Progress chasing   to keep all stages on time and warn quickly of any hold-ups

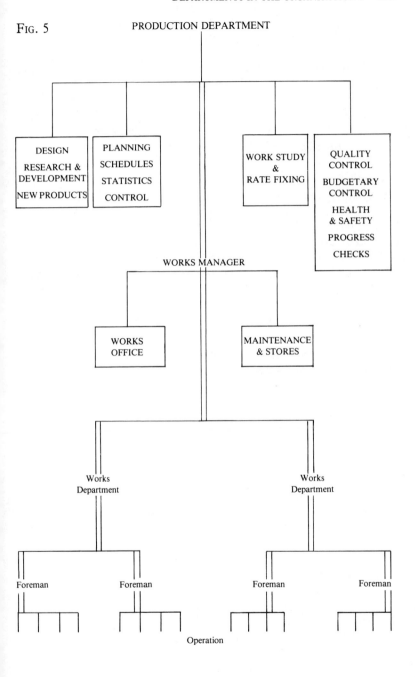

Fig. 5

4. Work-study   to ensure efficient practice
5. Health and safety   to ensure compliance with required precautions
6. Personnel   to ensure adequate supply and standard of labour and diagnose training requirements.

Overseeing the whole operation will be the production and works management, who must watch efficiency, seek improvements and exercise the time-honoured skills of leadership, foresight and creativity.

Marketing
Marketing is dealt with more fully in chapter 20. In simple terms, its purpose is to assess the market possibilities, using the information provided by the market research section, to establish the nature and quantity of demand and produce sales forecasts on which the company's activities will be based in the future. Through the sales force, advertising and sales promotion, marketing will ensure that the maximum profitable volume of the goods will be sold, and this is obviously the fundamental purpose. What is less obvious is its role in deciding the nature of the goods to be made. Marketing works on the proposition that before anything is made it is necessary to find out what and how much people will buy. Much of marketing responsibility is in this area as well as in that of selling and promoting the resultant product.

Design department
The design department is primarily concerned with the product, and incidentally with its appearance for advertising purposes.
    The design department must formulate goods on four main bases:

1. *The inherent efficiency of the product*
   It must work well, be adequately durable and preferably better in performance than competitive products. Designers must be alive to new materials, colours, shapes, styles and other aspects of design.

2. *Ease of production*
   The design department is not generally concerned with the layout or organisation of work within the factory, which belongs to work study or works management, but in drawing blueprints for products it must take account of new materials and constantly seek

to improve the product itself and the production process in the factory. Better design can often result in better work flow.

3. *Attractiveness*
Provided conditions (1) and (2) are not violated (and sometimes even if they have to be!) design is very much concerned with the appearance of the product, whether for aesthetic or eye-catching reasons. Again, new materials, colour schemes and shapes and the latest 'pop' or cultural ideas will be a strong influence.

4. *Novelty*
Newness is a feature of commercial success and the designs may be able to incorporate various unusual features, 'trendy' ideas and new materials. Pneumatic furniture is a good example.

The design department does not work in a vacuum. From market research it can get information about what people want, or think important, and what they find unsatisfactory in present products. From this source it will also get an idea of the number of people in a particular market: it may even have some of its designs tested for customer reaction in the early stages.

It works closely with the advertising department, which is usually full of ideas of its own and will later arrange all the publicity for the design department's creations. Often the advertising department will ask the designers to try and incorporate certain 'advertisable' features into the blueprints.

Not least, it will work closely with the production department, to incorporate the benefits of new production techniques, new materials, new scientific inventions, and to avoid products which, though attractive, may be unnecessarily complicated or expensive to make.

Design has a vitally important role in both production and marketing. That is why it is linked to both in Figure 4. Good design is essential to the nation's commercial success and the Council for Industrial Design and the Design Centre are both active in promoting it.

Personnel department
This is a functional department dealing with the recruitment of labour, its efficiency, training and satisfaction in work, and also with various aspects of welfare and medical care.

It can be divided into five main sections:

1. *Employment*

The personnel department helps management to formulate its employment policy and recruit labour, by keeping in contact with the sources of supply, namely the Job Centres and other agencies, and by the utilisation of advertising.

Having attracted applicants the personnel manager will be responsible for their interview, selection, and the terms of their engagement. After this he must appoint them to suitable posts, arrange any training that is necessary immediately or at later stages of their career with the firm. Ultimately, he may be concerned with the termination of their employment. Once they are established in the organisation, employees will have properly maintained records, regular reports giving gradings and merit-ratings, which will affect future promotion and increments in pay. These, together with statutory regulations regarding the employment of apprentices and young persons, the hours of work and overtime permitted (especially to females), are all the responsibility of this department.

2. *Remuneration*

A part of the company's employment policy will be the company's wage structure. The assessment and control of differentials between grades of employees, and the regular or specially merited rises which workers may earn are essential incentives for the work force. Personnel must work closely with Organisation and Methods and work-study specialists to ensure that new work patterns result in adequate rewards so that the operatives feel impelled to work well at the crucial tasks. It is also usually an interest of this department, in agreement with the individuals concerned, to authorise any deductions from their pay, e.g. for holiday fund, loans and indeed to some extent for their pension scheme.

3. *Industrial relations*

Personnel is initially concerned with the good of the company rather than that of the worker, but the common good of the two is so closely allied that the employee can regard a good personnel department as looking after his interests.

The personnel manager acts as the company's negotiating officer with the trade unions. He must have an extensive knowledge of conciliation and arbitration procedures, and be deeply involved with all forms of joint consultation and industrial psychology. He will help organise the works council and maintain and improve procedures for ventilating and dealing with workers' grievances.

Above all he must promote understanding of the company's personnel policy and interpret it in given situations.

4. *Medical and health*
In this sphere personnel is concerned with:

(*a*) the provisions of the Health and Safety at Work Act 1974 and other relevant regulations;
(*b*) maintaining means of contact with the factory inspector;
(*c*) maintenance of factory medical services including medical examination for employees, young people and new starters; maintenance of medical records;
(*d*) supervision of hazardous jobs;
(*e*) organising sick visiting and arranging for convalescence. In addition it may have under its control the safety officers, reporting of accidents to factory inspectors and the enforcement of safety regulations within the scope of the Health and Safety at Work Act.

5. *Welfare*
This division is concerned with:

(*a*) organisation of the canteen;
(*b*) sick club and benevolent fund;
(*c*) long service grants;
(*d*) pension funds and leaving grants;
(*e*) loans;
(*f*) legal aid;
(*g*) help with personal problems;
(*h*) housing and other accommodation;
(*i*) social and recreational facilities;
(*j*) time-off requests.

The work of the personnel department is vital to an efficient firm, because employees respond to a fair and just organisation, require a clear-cut career structure and need the means to discuss their grievances. Above all, in a very large company, they need some reassurance that they are regarded as individuals and human beings, not just as so many cogs in the machine.

The company secretary

Every company must have its official company secretary. He or she is not to be confused with a private secretary of any executive.

The company secretary is usually a qualified member of the Institute of Chartered Secretaries and Administrators. His function is semi-legal, for he is there to ensure that all the company's activities conform to the Memorandum and Articles of Association and to the Companies Act generally. The regular meetings of the board of directors and the Annual General Meeting must conform to established procedures and the company secretary will ensure that these are observed. With the chairman or managing director he will prepare the agenda and the summons to meetings, ensuring they are despatched to give due notice. He is responsible for the company's minute books and ensures that all such records receive the chairman's signature. He also has charge of the company's official seal used on legal documents.

In addition, he will keep the Register of Directors and of Shareholders, Debentures and Share Transfers. He must ensure that documents and returns are filed with the Registrar of Companies according to statutory requirements. The issue of shares, their transfer and the overseeing of the payments of dividends are all within his province. Above all, he is a source of advice and guidance to the directors on regulations and company procedure. Irregularities or negligence in complying with regulations and the Companies Acts and in the relationship of the company with the public can involve the company secretary in heavy fines and penalties, for his is the task of ensuring that correct and stated procedures which safeguard the shareholders and public are properly observed.

A full-time company secretary may be in charge of office services as an extension of his particular duties, but these are an additional and not an essential part of his official role.

The buying and stock control department

The contribution of this department can be the difference between the prosperity or failure of a business. Money lost through inefficient buying can offset the gains of improved production or the profits on thousands of pounds of sales. The savings achieved by shrewd buying or the eradication of stock losses can be added to the profits or used to make the firm's goods more competitive.

What is bought?
Goods and services are bought either for resale (as in the case of a shop or a wholesaler, or a travel agent), or (in the case of a manufacturer) to process them and sell the resultant products. All firms buy goods to maintain their activities, apart from the raw materials and components of their product and they include:
Operational supplies: oil, fuel, stationery.
Equipment: machines, typewriters, furniture, fittings.
Services: e.g. telephone, window-cleaning, press-cutting service, consultancy, hire of equipment, travel and insurance.

How does the buyer find out where to obtain the various articles?
It is the buyer's job to know the sources of supply and observe all relevant new ideas, improvements and materials, for they are essential to competitive buying. Such information is drawn from advertisements, brochures, catalogues, price lists and visiting salesmen. In addition, classified directories, informative articles in the trade press and discussion with other buyers will help. Direct enquiry to trade and professional associations or to the Chamber of Commerce is another method.

How does the buyer decide what to buy?
Some of the goods he buys will be requisitioned in specific terms from the other departments of the business. The production manager may ask for nuts and bolts of precise size and tensility. Indeed, the closest consultation with this and other departments is necessary in buying machinery and material, so that specialist knowledge and requirements are taken into account. Apart from these considerations of suitability the buyer will weigh the advantage of price, quality, delivery dates, cost of carriage and terms of payment (credit facilities), and cash discounts. Less tangible but not less important is his examination of the stability of the proposed supplier, his reliability and way of doing business.

How does the buyer order?
The buyer may order by letter, formal contract, or, most commonly, on the official order form of the firm. In the latter case there will be several carbon copies, particularly for the accounts department, the

stock controller and the requisitioning department. For convenience or quickness, some orders may be given orally by telephone, over the counter, or to visiting salesmen, but good practice will demand that a confirmation on the firm's official order will follow.

The buyer's activities in relation to the rest of the business
The buyer may purchase goods only if the company can afford them. So he must work in co-operation with the accounts department and keep within a planned budget. Since the accounts department must pay the bills for his purchases, procedures must be installed to ensure that the accounts department can be certain that bills presented are valid. This is the reason for sending copy orders to the accountant and why all incoming invoices must be verified by the buying department before they are paid. Methods must be developed:

1. to ensure that the goods have been received;
2. to ensure that they are the right goods and are up to specification; the buyer may have laboratory facilities for quality testing;
3. to ensure that the quantities are correct;
4. to ensure that goods received were in fact ordered, that the prices, discount, cost of carriage or containers are agreed and, not least, that no duplication of payment is possible.

The buyer, therefore, has the responsibility to see that he purchases competitively, that he keeps all departments aware of new and possibly more efficient products and that the terms of his bargaining in quality and in cost are carefully observed.

Stock control
Bad buying can be ruinous but over- or under-buying can be equally damaging, so the buyer must base his activities on a good stock control system.

If he buys too little, the factory may come to a standstill for lack of supplies, or he may have to buy in haste at the wrong (expensive) time and lose discounts on bulk buying.

If he buys too much, valuable capital may be tied up needlessly; space will be needed to store the goods, and bigger warehouses; the cost of handling, insurance and care will be greater; there is greater possible loss from damage, deterioration and pilferage.

Activities of stock control department

From the chart below it will be seen that the receipt, care and issue of stock are the chief responsibilities. The maintenance of stock records will provide:

1. the current stock balance at any time;
2. the indication of excessive or dangerously low levels at any moment;
3. discrepancies, fraud or pilferage.

The records must be checked regularly by physical stocktaking. True statements of stock and its valuation are essential to the company's balance sheet, and a false statement of stock can produce a quite

Fig. 6   ACTIVITIES OF STOCK CONTROL DEPARTMENT

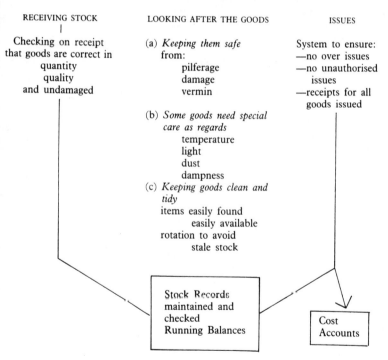

RECEIVING STOCK	LOOKING AFTER THE GOODS	ISSUES
Checking on receipt that goods are correct in quantity quality and undamaged	(a) *Keeping them safe* from: pilferage damage vermin	System to ensure: —no over issues —no unauthorised issues —receipts for all goods issued
	(b) *Some goods need special care as regards* temperature light dust dampness	
	(c) *Keeping goods clean and tidy* items easily found easily available rotation to avoid stale stock	

Stock Records maintained and checked
Running Balances

Cost Accounts

erroneous impression. With the annual balance sheet the managing director must sign a certificate affirming that the stocks and their valuation are correctly stated.

It will be observed that the inflow of stock is of importance to the accountant for reasons of payment, liquidity and balance sheets. The cost accountant also must be informed of all issues and the cost of stock because all material used in manufacture or repair must be priced and added to the cost of labour and overheads in order to arrive at the correct price to charge for the finished article. The cost accountant will keep a careful check that the real usage in production corresponds to the costed and planned quantities. If, for example, more platinum is being used for the manufacture of X number of electrical points than was planned then something (very costly) is wrong. Either the original planning was inaccurate (and so the selling price is wrong too) or some waste or pilferage can be suspected.

Stock control records can take many forms
Today many firms use computers. This is a straightforward and simple use of their high-speed tabulating capability. In essence, stock records are based on a starting balance plus incoming goods, minus goods issued and a resultant current balance. This can be seen from the simple visible stock card illustrated. All that is needed is accuracy, enough time and a will to take pains to keep such records up to date.

The last column can be used to calculate usage per month or for

Fig. 7

SIMPLE STOCK CARD

ITEM 6lb Hammers		Code No.	Minimum Stock 50	Maximum Stock 150	BIN No. . . .
Date	Order No.	Issue Vo. No.	Quantity In	Quantity Out	Running Balance
1.1.87	Brought	Forward			40
3.1.87	CY 3491		100		140
10.1.87		WN 41		7	133
30.1.87		WN 83		4	129
16.2.87		WX 109		12	117

remarks. The reverse of the card can record orders placed, the names, addresses, and prices of the suppliers and be used to check any undelivered orders. Symbols can be attached to the card to indicate minimum and maximum levels.

Transport and physical distribution department

Transport is an essential function in most businesses. Products are little use in the factory and must be delivered to the customer or to the shops he visits. Since the ultimate price of an article must include the cost of delivery, it is essential that the service should be organised efficiently, not only for the facilities it offers, but also for economy.

The main requirements for good transport may include:
economy;
speed;
safety and regularity of service;
flexibility to meet immediate or special needs;
freedom from damage;
cleanliness, hygiene and possibly special equipment (such as refrigeration or tail hoists).

Not all products require the same facilities and it is important to distinguish what is really necessary. For example, the need for cleanliness and refrigeration when carrying ice-cream does not apply when hauling coal: and the speed which is essential to convey fish from the ports, or daffodils from the Scilly Isles would be unnecessarily costly in providing a regular supply of china clay for the Potteries.

Some of these qualities are clearly in conflict. Speed fights with economy, and so does flexibility. If flexibility means having a spare van to meet customers' emergencies, this may be commercially desirable, but it is not economical fleet operation. So the transport manager must first work out (with the appropriate departments and notably with the marketing director) what are the requirements for the services and plan accordingly.

He can provide transport by:
1. using public hauliers casually or on contract;
2. using public services, railways, canals, ships, airlines, the Post Office for parcels and even possibly pipelines;
3. running his own fleet.

Alternatively he may use an appropriate combination of all three and it is the duty of the transport manager to choose the most economical or effective blend.

Export

Today many organisations will be involved in overseas trade and this places an additional burden of expertise on the transport department. It must cope with increased documentation, procedures at ports and those governing containers and trailers sealed by Customs at the factory for transcontinental traffic. Here, of course, there will be interdepartmental liaison with the export manager.

The company transport fleet

This is costly to run, but nevertheless offers savings in one direction and readily available transport which is entirely at the company's disposal.

In this case the transport manager must:

1. work out the size and most suitable types of vehicles for the work;
2. organise regular maintenance of the vehicles;
3. hire, pay wages and expenses and organise work of the drivers; this will include schedules and routes for delivery;
4. conform to the mass of statutory regulations governing the keeping and operating of commercial vehicles—MOT tests, insurance, licences, drivers' work tickets and permissible hours of work, including tachograph records;
5. maintain and examine the statistics of vehicle costs, the volume of goods they carry and so arrive at the most economical methods of delivering the goods on time;
6. be responsible for the purchase and policy for company cars for those grades of staff entitled to them.

His work may also include the control and operation of depots and indeed of the physical stock and central warehouses. In the latter case some of his activity would include part of the work outlined in the section on stock control.

Scheduling and organisation of deliveries

Whatever means of transport is chosen, there will be plenty of paper work. Delivery schedules and loading sheets must be prepared, so that vehicles cover the correct routes with their proper loads. Sometimes the returning vehicles may be able to pick up goods required for the factory from the suppliers, thereby saving something on the price of, for example, raw materials. Documentation to provide proof of delivery must be prepared, the drivers being instructed to obtain signatures; they may also be required to obtain payment for the present or previous consignments.

Apart from the sales staff, transport personnel have the closest general contact with the customer. Theirs is almost the last process in the chain of production and it is easy to offend or please by both personality and service. The customer wants his goods promptly, undamaged and as cheaply as possible. Failure to meet his needs quickly and courteously causes offence. Transport, therefore, is an important department in the organisation.

19

DEPARTMENTS IN THE ORGANISATION II

Accounts department
This is obviously concerned with the financial aspects of the organisation, the main aspects of which are as follows:

1. *The Financial accounts*
   The department will produce the annual balance sheet, including the profit and loss account, for presentation to the shareholders and which must be filed with the Registrar of Companies. In addition it may provide half-yearly, quarterly or monthly accounts for use of the board and the management. This type of accounting shows not only the trading position, but the disposition of the assets and finances of the organisation at a given time.

2. *Management accounts*
   A great deal of the chief accountant's work is concerned with the management of the firm's finances. He will be concerned with the availability of capital for proposed extension of activities, plant and buildings, and will offer advice on the way in which funds may be obtained or made available from existing resources. He will be concerned with ratios, such as return on capital, profit to sales, and with the relative profitability of the various enterprises in which the firm is engaged. He will thus be able to provide the management with facts and figures on which to judge the merits of proposals for new and the continuance of existing ventures as the best means of using the firm's resources.

3. *Receipt of money*
   Any organisation requires payment for its services or products. To ensure this, the accounts department must supervise the method by which an order is turned into the despatch of goods, and thence to the creation of invoices. The invoice is the primary device by which the sales ledger and record of debtors is built up. Adjustments to customers' accounts may be effected by further invoices or credit

166

notes. At the end of each accounting period the department must despatch statements of accounts in order to obtain the money due. It is the duty of this department to ensure prompt payment and to pursue overdue accounts, so that no long-term debtors exist or, worse still, bad debts. As a part of this work, careful credit control and scrutiny of new customers for credit-worthiness will be instituted.

4. *Payment of money*

It is important that a careful system for the payment of the company's debts should be developed and maintained. Any organisation has a mass of regular and casual bills to be paid, including those for rent, rates, fuel, services such as telephones and for all the goods and raw materials purchased. Care must be taken to ensure (a) that no bills are paid unless the goods have been received in total and in the quality specified, (b) that no bills are paid twice and (c) that the bills are in the terms and discounts agreed by the buyer.

A purchase ledger must be kept to record such debits, and when the bills are paid the sums must be charged to the various purposes for which the goods were purchased, whether for production, maintenance or more permanent items such as machines and furniture which remain as assets of the firm and must be catalogued as such.

Costing

A very distinct type of accountancy is concerned with the analysis of the costs of the various activities and products of the organisation. It is easy enough to estimate the cost of gold and diamonds in each diamond ring produced; but it is more difficult to determine what proportion of the fuel, design and telephone bills and indeed the managing director's Rolls Royce should be charged to each ring. Without the work of the cost accountant it is difficult to obtain a realistic idea of the true cost of producing the firm's product or service, and without this information, which incidentally will vary with the volume of production, it is difficult to operate efficiently and sell at competitive prices in the market.

No less important is the cost accountant's ability to isolate areas of excessive cost and to produce figures to show the relative expense of all activities, so that economies or increased expenditure can be approved according to the value of each and to the total well-being of the firm.

Wages and cashier

It is not absolutely essential that the wages department should come under the accountant, but generally it does. Wages require a close liaison with the other departments in order to ensure an inflow of essential information, such as overtime, bonuses (of critical interest to the cost accounting section), promotions, pension contributions and so forth. National Insurance and PAYE records and deductions must be made, and eventually payment made to each employee in cash or by cheque or credit transfer. In a big organisation this will require security arrangements, not only for money but also to ensure that the right people draw their wages.

The wages department must also administer the Statutory Sick Pay Scheme, and it is responsible likewise for paying over to the Inland Revenue PAYE deductions from wages and the national insurance contributions from employer and employees.

The cashier usually occupies a distinct position in the accountant's department, for he is responsible for handling money in cash and cheques. The preparation of cheques for payment, the receipt of cash and cheques for goods and services rendered, the disbursement of small cash sums for expenses and other matters, and the strict surveillance of petty cash accounts are all his concern. He must ensure that there is a foolproof system for scheduling money received in the post and channelling it eventually into the bank. He will usually also be responsible for the reconciliation of the bank statement.

Statistics and computers

All departments have a use for statistics. Properly collected and skilfully interpreted, they are the basis for objective—as opposed to subjective—decisions, and the inescapable record of performance for comparison with what was planned. As such, they are essential for control by management.

For example, the personnel department will keep records of sickness and absence (the number of occasions, the hours, the time of year, the departments concerned, and the types of disability). From this can be deduced how much time and money was lost, in what seasons absence can be expected, and what departments and processes are prone to certain illnesses. In such matters as job evaluation, wage-bargaining, industrial relations, and staff turnover—which indicates the state of morale, management efficiency, recruitment and selection techniques, not to mention safety and legal obligations—statistical evidence is fundamental.

Statistics must be collected properly

Statistics must be correct, relevant and complete. Bias, extraneous or inadequate data breed error and false conclusions. What is wanted is 'The truth, the whole truth and . . .'

The mechanics of statistics collection must be efficient and economic or the information can be too dearly bought. Good methods of 'once only' writing on skilfully designed forms with carbon copies will direct information into the statistics bank. Good organisation in recording detail can save work. If you add up all the males and all the females in a group the sum of the two totals will be the grand total of the group. This is better than first adding up all the people and then returning to the figures to analyse details of sex.

Statistics—processing the figures

The straightforward tabulation of figures into significant groups is often enough for management purposes. The conversion of totals into percentages, or ratios, is within the arithmetical capability of most clerical workers.

Statistics in the hands of qualified statisticians, however, can be used for forecasting, indexing, sampling and a host of other purposes to reduce the guesswork in managerial decisions.

Should there be a separate statistics department?

Clearly, the need for many or very advanced statistical skills suggests the idea of this function's being centred in one department. This could be fed with data from other departments, and could, in return, service them with regular and specified tabulations and analyses. After all, accountancy, which is a form of statistics, does exactly this.

The problem is not unlike the familiar one of choosing between central or departmental filing. The advantages of gathering together all statistical work at a single central point are the concentration of skills, economy of equipment—but not necessarily of communication, the avoidance of duplication and the comprehensive nature of the information collected. Against this must be set the loss of other benefits which result when individual departments deal with their own statistics—for example, the convenience of having material to hand, the specialised approach on departmental matters and the insights which department members have into their own facts and figures.

Highly technical centralised sections as described above can alienate a department from its own figures. The very skill and expertise of the statistician can be forbidding, and inhibit departments from a familiarity with their own data.

Nevertheless, organisations have a basic stream of figures relevant to all departments, and it is possible that the common good is greater than at first appears. Marketing figures and projections are, clearly, of great interest to all departments, and access to this information can generate ideas, economy and better relationships.

However, such a proliferation of figures was often costly, slow and suffocating, until the introduction of the punch-card systems and computers.

Computers

To a great extent the computer, and its predecessor the punch-card system, solved many problems. Both were expensive and cumbersome, needed skilled attention and could be operated only from a special department. On the other hand, they could absorb and process information very quickly and in great quantities.

Moreover, if, for example, the detail on an invoice were punched on to a card or tape it could be kept and as much or little tabulation, etc. as required taken off it at any time. There was no need to process all the information at once, and subsequent runs could use the data for varying purposes.

Computers went further. They could absorb the punch information into internal memories from which relevant details could be extracted automatically, used, and even amended as part of the programme.

Early computers were massive and inflexible. The new generation are powerful and capable of many times more work and have access points allowing input and retrieval of information by the departments and by all grades of staff. In addition, desk computers permit ancillary activity and experiment.

The computer scene changes quickly and today's authentic statement is quickly outdated and misleading, but certain problems and conceptions deserve consideration.

First, the introduction of a computer into any organisation requires thought. It may displace staff and processes or cause them to be re-allocated. It may cause frustration and fear among employees, and dislocation of procedures. The first stage must be an exercise in systems analysis and feasibility, so that the machines are properly and fully used and the staff know how their work fits in and who, if anyone, is at risk.

Secondly, the organisation needs careful formulation, so that the computer does not become a 'football' in office politics. Responsibility to—and for—the computer department is a most important factor. Restrictive attitudes and competitiveness between different departments can impede the response to change that very valuable technology demands.

Thirdly, the scope of the computer's activity must be clearly defined. It may, perhaps, be limited to a role purely in marketing or accounting or, at the other extreme, it may be used for a totally integrated system in which every activity, asset and policy of the company is included.

If a totally integrated data system is created, other problems must be faced. Because much of the information stored may be restricted and confidential, keys have to be devised to limit the access of staff to certain data. Security must be organised to prevent the disclosure of information to the outside world.

The inter-relationship of departments in the organisation

While it has been useful to examine departments individually, it must be understood that unless they are all properly integrated into the parent organisation—to serve, and be served by the other sections— their existence is meaningless.

Departments can easily become self-centred, and lose sight of their true purpose. They may become competitive and antagonistic, because of ambitious managers and staff anxious to defend their job security. Perhaps, more worthily, they seek perfection and discipline in procedure or paper work, and allow these to become more important than the service they are meant to provide. Absurdities can result, with customers being unable to place an order, or vital repairs being delayed, merely because a form is incomplete, or a cherished procedure has been breached.

Co-operation between departments does not occur naturally. It must be the conscious task of senior management to insist on it and foster the spirit of working as a team.

Good communication helps to maintain a clear understanding of corporate aims and current activity. If a little imagination is used in reporting the contributions of various departments to a project, will demonstrate not only the value of their work, but the superior importance of the overall task.

When a department is involved in planning for current or future operation, the contribution and interdependence of departments is most readily apparent. In fact, as Figure 8 shows, the high degree of participation in new schemes, and of repercussion from them is marked throughout the sections of the organisation. Study of this figure will reveal that the real significance and fulfilment of departments stems from the interplay between them, rather than from each one pursuing its own inward-looking excellence.

For example, the true purpose of the personnel department is to provide management with an adequate, properly trained and contented staff to implement the company's present and future policy. This may involve recruitment, engagement, redundancy, career development, training, labour relations, wage-bargaining, safety matters and legal conditions of employment. Great expertise is needed and the staff are wholly occupied by their work. Yet it is only valuable in the sense that it serves other sections and meets the objectives of the organisation as a whole. Equally, however, to discharge its obligations efficiently, the department must have full knowledge of the company's intentions for the future. It is a practical, rather than an ideal, requirement that the department should take part in the earliest stages of planning to advise on proposals and participate in innovating schemes, besides contributing later in their implementation.

Figure 8 gives some idea of the repercussions which a marketing proposal may have on other departments.

The example given can be applied to other functionaries, such as the buyer, the office manager, the packaging and export department. Even the gatehouse staff and the company secretary will be involved. The latter may be called on for architectural plans, contracts and land deeds, local government requirements—if premises are required—in addition to patents, trade marks and registration of names.

The marketing department, which started all this, will need to exchange ideas, provide estimates and timing of demand. The department may also have to adapt its proposals if, in the factory discussions, difficulties are foreseen or improvements suggested. It, in its turn, will rely on the factory for prompt production and extras, such as samples.

The basis for most commercial organisations, and public bodies, is an investment to produce articles or services, and market them at a

Fig. 8

A company proposes to introduce a major new product which may require more capital and/or some of the factory capacity now in use for other products. All departments are likely to be affected, with consequent problems and opportunities. For example:

ACCOUNTANCY
Financial
Management
Cost and Works
Book-keeping

Problems Provision of capital for research and development, raw materials, stocks, labour, machines, and debtors. Possibly for major items of new plant or factory buildings.

Decisions regarding best sources e.g., debentures, overdraft or share issue. Advice on various ratios, D.C.F., etc. Additional work for accountancy services; invoicing, costings, wage payments and bonuses. May be a lag in profit on investment.

Hopes Additional profit, spread of risk. Larger department with chance to reorganise and sort out under-employed staff and processes. Good excuse to review departments and company.

PRODUCTION

Problems Adequacy of factory space and amenities.

Adequacy of staff skills, numbers and deployment.

New raw materials and processes to be proved and run in.

Programming with variation of processes: stops and starts.

Advice required on the product, its development, difficulties in production, possible improvements.

Hopes May take up static or vacant factory capability.

Will be uncomplicated (can advise on how to avoid difficulty and get best arrangement).

Will have long runs with little or no changes.

Will help spread factory overheads.

continued

TRANSPORT and DISTRIBUTION Warehouses Depots Loading Materials handling Documentation	*Problems* Additional product to stock, identify, stock-take, load, schedule, insure. May require more space and greater security. May need special handling or special vehicles, or purchase of additional lorries. Alternatively new contracts or requirements for carriage may need negotiation. Need to advise on handling, packing and storage. *Hopes* May mean fuller vehicles and more economical loads. Opportunity to get some new vehicles and reorganise fleet, depots and warehousing.

Discuss the impact of such a change on personnel, statistics, buying, the secretarial and office services, and any other aspect of the organisation you can think of. Then try the effect on departments of a cut in production, or the discontinuance of a product or service.

profit—or for public benefit. The two main line departments are production (or buying for merchants) and marketing, which must be completely inter-dependent. They are serviced and monitored by other departments, which increase their efficiency, and competitiveness, and exist only to do this. To counterfeit a phrase, 'No department is an island . . .'

20

MARKETING

The ultimate aim of all business activity is to achieve a profit which is normally distributed on a basis similar to the following:
1. dividends to shareholders—the suppliers of capital who thus make possible the business activity;
2. interest on loans to debenture holders (a special class of investor with whom secured loans are arranged as distinct from the investment made by shareholders in the purchase of the company's shares on the stock market);
3. interest to banks and finance houses for temporary loans obtained by the company;
4. the retention, or ploughing back, of profits in order to build up a capital reserve for future development projects within the business.

Profits can only come from revenue, and revenue is the result of selling and obtaining orders for the company's products or services.

There is an old, but very true, adage 'nothing happens until somebody sells something'. To sell and to obtain the order for the company's products or services is a logical and necessary sequel to all the previous activity undertaken in the field of research and experiment, leading to productivity. These activities without the ultimate sales, however, would result in complete financial chaos and failure for the company. On the success of the salesman depends not only his own personal progress, but the success and progress of the company, and the maintenance of full employment for the workpeople of every grade in every department.

Selling is the ultimate aim of the marketing department and, therefore, it is desirable to consider, in some detail, the function of marketing in the average kind of business.

Marketing defined
Marketing is defined by the Institute of Marketing in the following terms:

'The management function which organises and directs all those business activities involved in assessing and converting customer purchasing power into effective demand for a specific product or service, and in moving the products or service to the final customer or user, so as to achieve the profit target or other objective set by a company.'

This fairly lengthy definition is widely accepted and interpreted in the business. Within the concept of that definition the marketing function follows a logical sequence of events which are now described:

1. *Market research*

   Before embarking on the manufacture and sale of a product it is important to assess the likely market for it and the best means of reaching that market. One must take into account the competition from other products, and discover the features which potential customers will find attractive enough to make them want to buy the article. Consumer reaction is tested by highly sophisticated research. Surveys are made to test the views of carefully chosen samples of the population. They may be selected by age, sex, area of residence, occupation and socio-economic group. The respondents are usually asked to complete a questionnaire. Teams of researchers conduct the enquiry, and the results are analysed. They will indicate the public's reaction to many features of the product. These may include its purpose, design, colour, size, appearance, shape, smell or taste (if applicable), price, packaging, convenience, availability and other aspects. If the indications are favourable, test-marketing may be carried out in small areas, before the main launch of a new product. Market research is also used to check the public's view of an established product if, for instance, the manufacturer is contemplating changes to boost sales.

2. *Advertising*

   Following a definite decision as to the nature of the product, including price and pack, based on market research, advertising would be the next stage. The obvious purpose of advertising is to draw attention to the merit, value and other virtues of the product with the fundamental aim of sales. Advertising is costly and, to be fully justified in terms of profits, must be directed skilfully at those potential purchasers who are regarded as being likely to be most keenly interested.

The prime decision in an advertising campaign is the medium or media to be employed. These advertising media may include press, posters or television.

Press.   The choice of newspapers and periodicals in the various categories:

nationals (daily and Sunday);

local (daily, evening and weekly);

trade papers.

special interest publications (specifically covering the likely readership for the product advertised, e.g., motoring, gardening, music, sport, handicrafts, etc.)

An important factor in the choice of any periodical is its certified circulation, which can be ascertained from advertising directories. (Most leading trade and specialist publications are members of the Audit Bureau of Circulations—an official body which will authenticate actual circulation figures.)

Posters.   Use of posters is the main form of *outdoor advertising.* The design and size of posters must be considered, and the most attractive positions for them, e.g., hoardings, railway stations, air terminals, bus stations, moving vehicles, such as buses and trains. A good example is the extensive and striking advertising on the London Underground on station walls, walls of escalators and inside the trains themselves. In this advertising the designers cleverly exploit the fact that members of the public travelling underground are not distracted to the same degree as they would be in the streets and are, therefore, able to give more attention to the advertisements displayed.

Sports grounds   A recent development in outdoor advertising is the promotion of brand names by the use of boards prominently displayed at football and cricket matches, and other sporting events. These are intended to catch not only the spectator's eye but also, and very deliberately, the television viewer's eye.

Direct mail.   This has traditionally been an effective and popular means of advertising and selling products and services. A skilfully compiled covering letter, with an attractive brochure—and, in some cases, competitions and free gift offers—can be sent to potential customers at a low cost per head. Many firms maintain their own mailing-lists, based on existing customers, sales records and the use of directories. Ready-made lists may be bought from specialist direct-mail firms. Advertising agencies will also provide assistance. Shrewd planning and tactics have, however, become important, because the growing use of this type of advertising and the insertion of leaflets in magazines has produced a degree of consumer-resistance to unsolicited 'junk mail'.

Cinema. Screen time in the intervals between main feature films is available to advertisers, for a fee. They have the advantage of a 'captive' audience, and a simple and effective way of getting their message across.

Television. This is probably the most expensive, but regarded generally as the most effective, medium for many products and services. Decisions will be needed on such essential factors as the extent of national or local coverage, choice of appropriate day and time to screen the advertisement. 'Peak' viewing times cost very much more than 'off peak' times. Television commercials have become very sophisticated and require specialist handling.

A 'watchdog', in the form of the Advertising Standards Authority, exists to maintain standards of honesty and decency. There is also a professional code of ethics within the industry, which is pledged to guard against fraud, misrepresentation and other undesirable practices.

3. *Public relations*

A public relations drive or campaign is often linked to the advertising campaign and may include press conferences at which prepared press releases are issued. The hope is that journalists and other media representatives will give the item free coverage—and therefore publicity—on the strength of its news value. A public relations campaign might also precede exhibitions at national and regional centres and might be used to publicise the launch of a new product, perhaps using well-known personalities.

4. Selling

It is, of course, assumed that linked with all the advertising and public relations activity there will already be enough products manufactured to allow a planned selling campaign to start as an *immediate* sequel to the advertising. An adequate supply of samples of all sizes should be ready for demonstrations and displays by retailers, departmental stores, etc. Each sales representative sets out on a carefully routed journey to introduce the new product to wholesalers and retailers and obtain initial orders. It may be necessary to train and appoint new or additional representatives and, for some products, where promotional aids and back-up material are desirable, merchandisers would be employed.

Sales force To be effective the sales force must be large enough to cover all the areas in which maximum sales are required. Each sales representative is allocated a territory which he is expected to cover systematically. Supervision is maintained by a sales director assisted by area sales managers, to whom the representatives are responsible for reporting progress and problems. Remuneration, ideally, should be by an adequate basic salary, commission on all orders from the territory and reimbursement of all legitimate expenses incurred on business journeys.

5. Merchandising

Merchandising is seen in many distributive trades as an essential link between advertising and selling. The *advertising campaign* will normally have been directed at the *public*, urging them to buy from the traders. The *selling campaign* is directed at the *traders*, persuading them to buy stocks to meet the demand. Merchandising operates to bring about the best possible display of the stocks purchased. Merchandising includes point-of-sale aids such as leaflets, showcards, window stickers and free samples. Merchandisers are usually regarded as a junior section of the sales force and are subject to the same degree of control as sales representatives, but their remuneration is normally restricted to salary with the reimbursement of expenses incurred on business journeys. The long-term importance of their work is increasingly being recognised by manufacturers in the distributive trades.

6. *Administration*

The staff of the sales office deals with customers' enquiries for samples, repeat orders and, where necessary, queries or complaints. The same staff deals with various administrative matters connected with sales representatives and merchandisers, namely salaries, incentive schemes, where necessary, reimbursement of expenses, allocation of sales territories, statistics and evaluation of the sales representatives' results.

7. *Transport*

Adequate transport arrangements are vital to ensure that orders are delivered as speedily as possible, either direct to the buyer by the company's own vehicles or to specified points for despatch by rail, air, sea or by haulage contractors.

8. *Export*

The development of export trade in the product obviously requires the appointment of able and qualified representatives to take part in international trade (or the appointment of foreign agents). Close attention must be paid to all the statutory requirements of successful export trading. For this the Export Promotions Department of the Department of Trade and Industry is helpful and valuable and this service can be obtained without difficulty from the DTI offices in London and provincial centres. (See Chapters 8 and 21.)

9. *Repeat orders*

The ultimate object of all marketing and selling activity is to obtain and ensure an adequate flow of repeat orders. In most businesses the real profit is on repeat orders. The profit on such orders offsets the high expense of launching a new product. Regular repeat orders over a prolonged period are, therefore, the recipe for success in any kind of business activity.

21

GOVERNMENT DEPARTMENTS AT WORK

The student of business is expected to know something of the work of those government departments (generally referred to as 'ministries') which have a direct influence on the business world. Chapter 8 of this book gives a general description of the principal departments.

The very wide range of government activity naturally has a considerable influence on the business world, but not all departments are directly involved with commerce and industry. Those which should be studied are the Department of Trade and Industry, the Department of Employment and the Treasury. The work of these three ministries, and their influence on Britain's commerce will be examined here, for the guidance of the student and for subsequent reference.

While it is always possible that changes will be made to government work and decisions—either during the lifetime of one government, or by a new government, following a General Election—the work of this group of ministries is so fundamental to the business world that any major change in their functions and general administrative work is unlikely.

Department of Trade and Industry
The team of ministers—all appointed by the Prime Minister of the day—is headed by the Secretary of State, who is by virtue of that office the President of the Board of Trade. Supporting the Secretary of State are three Ministers of State, one for Trade, one for Industry and one for Information Technology. Each is assisted by a Parliamentary Under Secretary. The department's activities are organised into divisions, each controlled by a senior civil servant responsible to the Secretary of State through one of the Ministers of State or Parliamentary Under Secretaries.

This team shares the department's work as three pairs (a Minister of State and a Parliamentary Under Secretary). While all members are ultimately responsible to the Secretary of State, they each carry a high degree of personal responsibility. This may entail being the spokesman for the department in Parliament, in matters connected with their particular division, receiving deputations, dealing with correspondence, carrying out external duties, such as visits at home and abroad, attending meetings and conferring with their opposite numbers from Commonwealth and foreign governments. All this is in addition to their work as Members of Parliament for their respective constituencies. (Perhaps their most important requirement in all this is a very efficient and well-trained private secretary!) It should be noted, in passing, that this description of a minister's duties applies equally to ministers in other government departments.

The work of the Department of Trade and Industry (DTI) falls, as the title indicates, under two main headings—one is trade and the other is industry—and in so far as influence on the business world is concerned it is described below.

Work relating to trade

Overseas trade
In this important field the department undertakes the promotion and protection of the overseas trading interests in a variety of ways. For each country concerned with exports from the United Kingdom there is a specific service to exporters, including advice on conditions in the appropriate overseas markets. The department is assisted by the British Overseas Trade Board, which consists of experienced businessmen and officials of the DTI, in supplying export information through the Board's London and regional offices and at overseas trade fairs.

There is also considerable co-operation with British embassies and consulates abroad in providing exporters with advice, information, assistance and any necessary technical help.

In selling to the export market there are various risks outside anyone's control. Some are the normal commercial kind, such as the inability of the purchaser to pay when the goods have been delivered; others could be of a political nature, such as unexpected disorder in a foreign country. These and all other risks can be covered by providing exporters with an insurance on a commercial basis; this is done by the Export Credits Guarantee Department which is responsible to the Secretary of State for its work.

Trade with the Common Market Countries involves the DTI in making available advice and help on all aspects of the special kind of international trading within the EEC.

Import trade is also a responsibility of one of the DTI divisions, covering such problems as the tariffs imposed by the government on certain goods coming into the country. These are known as protective tariffs, since they are designed to protect the home trade from unfair competition. Some imports must have an import licence before being unloaded, and this aspect is administered by the department, which is here guided by certain anti-dumping laws made from time to time by the government. In all this work, the department represents the government in the activities of the General Agreement on Tariffs and Trade (GATT) and the United Nations Conference on Trade and Development (UNCTAD) and liaison takes place with the appropriate departments of other governments.

Company law

The wide range of company law affects the day-to-day work of almost every business, large or small. Its object is to prevent malpractice and protect shareholders in companies. The Companies Act places responsibilities on company directors, and on company secretaries, and state penalties for non-compliance. Shareholders, being members of the company, have legal rights, such as attendance at general meetings and the right to vote there—including the important right to vote in the election of directors. Any shareholder who considers himself or herself prevented from exercising any of the rights granted under company law may request the department to intervene.

The department has a Companies Legislation Division which handles the administration of company law including its review from time to time, and the linking of company law with that operating in the Common Market. The division is responsible for the work of the Companies Registration Office, to which full details of every company must be sent by the company secretary. Important among the division's duties is the operation of the Protection of Fraud (Investors) Act, Protection of Depositors Act, and other measures to protect investors in unit trusts.

A company may come to the end of its existence by what is known as being 'wound up'. The winding-up may be 'voluntary' or 'compulsory', the difference being whether of not the directors have control of the winding-up of the company's affairs. In some cases a voluntary winding-up takes place because the purposes of the company have ceased to exist and the company remains solvent. In that event, the assets of the company are realised and the proceeds shared out between the shareholders.

A compulsory winding-up usually takes place because a company becomes insolvent and creditors force the company to close down. A liquidator, usually an accountant, is appointed to take charge of the company's affairs, realise what is left of the company's assets and pay the shareholders a dividend according to their respective shareholdings.

In some cases creditors do not insist on an immediate winding-up, and the appointment of a liquidator, but try instead to keep the company in operation for as long as may be necessary to recover sufficiently from the insolvency to pay off the creditors. In those cases the creditors appoint a receiver, usually an accountant, to take charge of the company's affairs, but with the object of enabling it to continue as a going concern for as long as may be necessary to meet the creditors' demands.

For small businesses which have not been formed into limited companies, the law of bankruptcy applies in the event of insolvency, in a similar manner to the provisions of company law.

All this creates a need for some form of government control. The DTI Insolvency Service administers all aspects of insolvency on the winding-up of companies under the Companies Acts, and the failure of businesses under the Insolvency and Bankruptcy Acts. Its duties include supervising the activities of liquidators and receivers. There are cases where the DTI intervenes by placing the insolvent concern in the hands of the Official Receiver, who is a senior civil servant appointed by the Official Receivers' Service of the DTI, which has offices in London and the regional centres.

Insurance

This is another field which inevitably concerns every commercial and industrial venture and requires some form of government control. The DTI is the authority responsible for administering the Insurance Companies Act. It authorises and supervises insurers, and its object is to ensure maximum protection and a fair deal, both for the business community and the individual policy-holder, in return for the vast amount spent each year on insurance premiums.

Monopolies and mergers

This is a subject frequently highlighted in the press because of its wide-ranging effects, both good and bad. A division of the DTI, with the title Competition Policy, Consumer Credit and Safety, covers a wide and important field. It concerns itself, for example, with government policy and legislation on monopolies, mergers, restrictive practices and various other aspects of business competition, together with consumer credit and consumer safety.

Consumer affairs

The protection of the consumer the general public, and particularly the individual retail shopper is assigned to the Consumer Affairs Division, which deals with government policy and legislation on general consumer matters, Consumer Councils, The Office of Fair Trading, whose director is appointed by the Secretary of State, weights, measures and metrication, including the problems of conversion from imperial to metric units, such as kilograms, metres, litres, etc.

Radio transmission

A division specialises in matters of radio frequencies, CB radio, cable and satellite transmission, licensing and radio interference.

Work relating to industry

Apart from its activities in connection with trade, the DTI has another wide range of responsibilities relating to industry. Those which have an influence on the business world are described below.

Regional assistance   There are very important reasons justifying government support of the regions throughout the UK to various degrees. Some regions are more prosperous than others; some have special geographical problems; some have declining industries, while others benefit from New Town and similar development.

Of special interest, therefore, is the Regional Selective Assistance Division, created under the Industrial Development Act. It deals with area promotion and publicity, designated 'assistance areas' and investment grants. It also sponsors tourism.

Sponsorship of industry   An interesting feature of the department's general work is the sponsorship —in the form of general government support and encouragement—for selected industries. Among these are:

Aircraft and aero-engines

Ship-building, marine equipment and hovercraft

Motor vehicles and motor cycles

Electronics, including industrial automation, computers, telecommunications, office machines, etc.

Minerals and metals—British Steel, private sector steel, and iron foundries

Chemicals, paper, etc., including textiles, man-made fibres, clothing, knitwear, footwear, plastics, pottery, cutlery and furniture

Small Firms Service   Government support for such firms, usually defined as undertakings with fewer than 200 workers, is reflected in the operations of this DTI body. It is run on a national and regional basis and offers a wide range of information and advice to people who contemplate setting up a small business. It deals with aspects such as drawing up a plan for the business, raising money to finance it, finding and choosing premises, planning, marketing and production.

As part of the advisory service there is a team of business counsellors, who are not civil servants, but experienced businessmen who are able to give sound and impartial advice on existing or proposed business projects.

Department of Employment

Of all the government departments, the Department of Employment has the greatest influence on the day-to-day work of the business world. Any firm, large or small, depends on its workers and employers and both categories come within the department's sphere. A general description of its work has already been given in Chapter 8.

The department administers and implements employment law. There has been a great deal in recent years, notably The Trade Union and Labour Relations Acts of 1974 and 1978, Contracts of Employment Act 1972, Employment Protection Act 1975, Employment Protection (Consolidation) Act 1978, and the Employment Acts of 1980 and 1982. This list of statutes shows the deep interest and concern of successive Parliaments in employment law, and Parliament may be expected to keep this law under continuous review, with further possible changes.

The ministerial team comprises a Secretary of State, who is a member of the Cabinet, a Minister of State, and two Parliamentary Under Secretaries. Because of the nature of their responsibilities and the public interest in them, these ministers are more often in the eye of the public and the media than those of other ministries.

The influence of the department on industry, commerce and business generally is exercised in the following areas.

Manpower Services Commission

The creation of the commission was a major step forward in operating the public employment and training services of the government, and developing a national manpower policy. The Commission is separate from the government, but answerable to the Secretary of State for Employment, and to the Secretaries of State for Wales and Scotland where appropriate. It has a chairman and nine members, all appointed by the Secretary of State for Employment after consultation with the TUC, CBI, and associations representing local government and education interests.

The commission has four main aims, namely:

1. To raise employment and lower unemployment
2. To develop manpower resources
3. To help in securing for workers a way 'towards a satisfying working life'
4. To 'improve the quality of decisions affecting manpower'

There are two main operating divisions of the Commission—Employment Service and Training Service. Their work is summarised below:

Employment Service Division   This gives help to workers in choosing, training for and obtaining the right work. It also helps employers to find the right workers speedily. Both services are available at local Employment Offices and Job Centres, together with a special service for disabled people.

The Professional and Executive Recruitment Service (PER) specialises in placing people at managerial, executive, professional, scientific and technical levels.

Employment Rehabilitation Centres provide courses for people wishing to enter, or re-enter, employment after sickness, injury or a long spell of unemployment.

Training Services Division   This division helps to develop a national training system to offer training skills for which there is a demand and to improve the standards of training. It contributes to the running of Industrial Training Boards and supports a number of training bodies not covered by the boards. It is also responsible for the Youth Training Scheme (YTS) (see page 206).

Health and Safety at Work Commission

The creation of this Commission and its composition resemble those of the Manpower Services Commission in that it is independent and yet answerable to the Secretary of State for Employment. It has to take appropriate steps to secure the health, safety and welfare of people at work and protect the public generally against risks to health or safety, arising out of their work and working conditions.

Membership of the Commission includes representatives of management, trade unions, and local authorities, and it provides a national forum for the discussion of health and safety policy. The Commission organises widespread consultation on all aspects of health and safety. It has a number of advisory committees and an executive arm—the Health and Safety Executive. Both the Commission and the Executive were set up under the provisions of the Health and Safety at Work Act 1974.

The Executive's dual role is to exercise on behalf of the Commission such of its functions as the Commission directs, and to make adequate arrangements for the enforcement of the health and safety legislation.

The law on responsibilities of employers and rights of employees regarding health and safety at work has been extended considerably by the Health and Safety at Work Act 1974, and the responsibilities of employers include the following:

Protection in the use of 'articles and substances at work'

Training in the technical hazards of particular work places, and on health precautions and safety

Creation of Safety Committees, with the appointment of safety representatives from the work-force, and their training as laid down in a Code of Practice published by the Executive.

Employers must, of course, take the prudent step of insuring against liabilities to their employees for injuries or diseases caused at work. Within the provisions of the Employers' Liability (Compulsory Insurance) Act 1972, this is compulsory, as is the display of a Certificate of Insurance at all branches of the employer's business where every employee can see and read it.

Advisory Conciliation and Arbitration Service
Equal Opportunities Commission
Commission for Racial Equality

While the work of these three bodies is governed by the Department of Employment, an account of the part played by each of them will be found in the later chapters of this book. (See Chapters 23 The Human Element and 22 Industrial Relations.)

Unemployment Benefit
In the payment of unemployment benefit at local Employment Offices, the Department of Employment is acting as the agent of the Department of Health and Social Security.

The Treasury
The main task of the Treasury has been described as the managing of the UK's economy so as to achieve objectives put forward by successive ministers and approved by Parliament. Despite the changes of government from time to time, there has usually been a wide measure of agreement as to what those objectives shall be. In general terms they are the achievement of a high level of employment, an acceptable rate of economic growth, reasonably stable prices, an equitable distribution of wealth and income and a satisfactory balance of payments.

The ministerial team at the Treasury consists of the Chancellor of the Exchequer, the Chief Secretary, the Financial Secretary, the Parliamentary Secretary and a Minister of State. Their various responsibilities and functions are shared out, as for the ministers in other departments.

Though the work of the Treasury is far-reaching and complex, the business student is primarily concerned with the influence the Treasury has in the business world. This inevitably leads on to the payment of tax in one or more of the various categories.

The Treasury has two departments responsible for the gathering of tax—the Inland Revenue and Customs and Excise. The official titles of these departments are: The Commissioners of Her Majesty's Inland Revenue, and The Commissioners of Her Majesty's Customs and Excise.

Inland Revenue   This deals with taxes such as Income Tax, Corporation Tax levied on company profits, Capital Gains Tax, Inheritance Tax, Development Land Tax, and Petroleum Revenue Tax.

In the case of income tax paid by employees under the PAYE (pay as you earn) system employers collect this, on behalf of the Inland Revenue, by deducting the tax due to be paid by the employee from his weekly or monthly wage or salary. The amount thus collected is paid over to the local office of the Inland Revenue at monthly intervals.

Customs and Excise This department is concerned with various other forms of tax, namely:

Customs Duty: The amount of duty levied on goods imported into the United Kingdom and collected by Customs Officers at the sea or air port of entry.

Excise Duty: A tax on the production of specified goods within the United Kingdom e.g., beer, spirits, tobacco goods.

Betting and Gaming Tax: A levy on gambling.

Vehicle Tax: Levied on all forms of motor transport.

Value Added Tax: VAT is a tax affecting all business activity not only in paying it, but also in collecting it, as will be seen from the following description.

Value Added Tax

The impact of VAT is very wide-ranging and although a complex subject, the operation of the tax is quite easy to understand. It is a tax on the sale of goods and services, conforming to EEC regulations, under which all member countries are obliged to operate a VAT system.   The Treasury regards VAT with favour. It has the great advantage not only of producing revenue, but of acting as an economy regulator. Changes in rates of VAT may be made at any time, for any reason the Treasury considers necessary. Such changes, however, are very infrequent. Normally changes of rate are introduced as part of tax changes made in the Chancellor of the Exchequer's annual budget which he presents to Parliament. The fact remains, however, that VAT rates may also be altered by Treasury Order under the provisions of the Finance Acts.

There is a stated VAT-free amount of turnover, which is increased by Treasury Order, usually at annual intervals, but when that amount is exceeded 'registration' with the VAT authorities is compulsory.

The 'person', not the business, must be registered. That 'person' may be a sole proprietor of a business, a partnership including a husband and wife partnership, a limited company, a club or association, etc. A group of limited companies may arrange a single registration.

Application for registration is made to the nearest VAT Office. There is usually one in or near every city and town, and that office will give all necessary guidance and help. When registration has been completed a VAT number is allocated, and from then on the number must be shown on all invoices, accounts statements and letterheads.

Many persons operating small businesses are outside the scope of VAT regulations, because their turnover is below the fixed minimum. Of course as turnover grows and reaches the critical figure VAT registration is obligatory.

Operation of VAT   The appropriate amount of tax is collected at *each stage* of the process of production or distribution of goods or services. The final tax is borne by the consumer or, in the case of services, the user—at the end of the line. All businesses need supplies in one form or another—raw materials, stock for re-sale, etc.—and the VAT paid by the business for such items is the *input tax*. Conversely, when the business proceeds to supply goods or services to *customers* it must *charge* VAT to those people. That process is known as 'output' and the VAT charged is *output tax*.

At prescribed intervals, usually three months, the business must send a statement to the Customs and Excise authorities on which are totalled respective amounts of output and input tax. If the amount of output tax is greater than the amount of input tax the balance is payable to Customs and Excise. If the opposite is the case, a refund is made to the business by Customs and Excise.

Rates of tax   The Treasury regulates the rates of VAT, and currently there is one rate known as the 'standard rate', although there have been times when a higher rate was charged on certain luxuries. There is also a range of goods and services which are the subject of a 'zero-rate', and another range which is exempt from VAT, as set out below:

1. *Zero rate* (Tax rate nil) includes
   Exports of goods
   Most international services
   Most food (excluding meals in restaurants, cafés, etc., and take-away food)
   Books and newspapers
   New buildings, building construction (excluding repairs and alterations)
   Mobile homes and houseboats
   Dispensing of prescriptions and the supply of many aids for the disabled
   Young children's clothing and footwear

2. *Exempt range* (No VAT charged) includes
Lettings and property leases of 21 years or less (excluding garage lettings, parking charges, hotel and holiday accommodation)
Insurance
Betting, gaming and lotteries (excluding gaming-machine takings, admission to premises, club subscriptions and certain participation charges)
Provision of credit
Education; professional and job-training
Services of doctors, dentists, opticians, etc.
Undertakers' charges for funerals
Membership fees to trade unions and professional bodies

There is an important difference between *zero* and *exempt* supplies. Supplies in the *zero rate* range count towards the turnover amount required for registration as explained above; supplies in the *exempt* range do not. Anyone concerned only with exempt supplies, therefore, cannot be registered for VAT.

Full details of *zero* and *exempt* ranges are set out in a VAT publication obtainable free of charge from any VAT Office. A wide range of other explanatory booklets covers such matters as imports, exports, hotels and catering, children's clothing and footwear.

The Home Office

A responsibility of the Home Office in the business world is the implementation of the Data Protection Act 1984. The scope of the Act is stated as 'To regulate the use of automatically processed information relating to individuals and the provision of services in respect of such information'. It applies to the users of their own computing equipment and to the services of computer bureaus. The term 'computer equipment' covers mainframe, mini and micro-computers as well as word processors.

The Act has created the office of Data Protection Registrar to implement the provisions of the Act, and all data users (the owners of computing equipment) and computer bureaus are required to make a registration with the office.

22

INDUSTRIAL RELATIONS

The benefits obtained from good industrial relations are becoming increasingly recognised by what is known as both sides of industry, that is, employers and management on one hand, and workers and their representatives, the trade unions, on the other.

Through harmonious management/worker relations, production, output and service can be kept at a high level, and pay and conditions of work made acceptable to employees of every grade and status.

Therefore, the need for the best possible industrial relations is recognised as having a very high priority. More and more employers, large and small, are becoming aware of this; trade unions, too, are seeing the benefits which good industrial relations can create for their members.

It is not surprising, therefore, that successive governments in recent years have given increasing attention to laws on industrial relations acceptable to both sides of industry and this will clearly continue to be a topic of discussion and debate.

The Department of Employment is responsible for the legislation—as was seen in the previous chapter—and the long list of statutes on various aspects of employment law is an indication of the deep and growing interest of Parliament in the whole subject of industrial relations.

Most of the law on the individual employee's rights is contained in the Employment Protection (Consolidation) Act of 1978, but there have been minor modifications in the Employment Acts of 1980 and 1982. As all this law is kept under review by the Department of Employment, it is always possible that further changes will be made. Accordingly the student must realise how necessary it is to keep up-to-date on this subject.

Advisory, Conciliation and Arbitration Service (ACAS)

One of the most important features of industrial relations work—if not the most vital—is the service available through ACAS. The service was set up under the Employment Protection Act 1975 by the Department of Employment, but is independent of the government or the Department of Employment in its work. Indeed, emphasis has been placed on the importance of the service's being entirely independent and not controlled by either side of industry.

The service is run by a council appointed by the Secretary of State for Employment. It consists of a chairman and nine members, three nominated by the Confederation of British Industry, three by the Trades Union Congress and three independent members. The staff consists of persons with special experience of industrial relations and many of its members are highly trained.

The service's primary aim is to help employers, workers and their representatives improve their relations with one another. It is recognised , of course, that direct responsibility for good relations rests with the parties involved—employers, workers and their representatives—but an independent third party, such as ACAS, with time and experienced staff available, can often help better understanding of a problem and bring the views of both sides closer together.

Specially trained industrial relations officers are based in London and regional offices. They can provide prompt confidential assistance over the whole field of industrial relations and employment problems, including matters such as payment systems and productivity schemes, settling disputes and grievances, trade union recognition, and training in industrial relations.

ACAS also provides conciliation in cases of complaint to Industrial Tribunals by employees alleging unfair dismissal and other infringements of employees' legal rights. By bringing the parties together, an experienced ACAS officer can often achieve an agreed settlement and so avoid a long, and perhaps difficult, Industrial Tribunal hearing.

Another important feature of the ACAS work is the provision of Codes of Practice giving practical guidance on various aspects of employment problems, such as disciplinary practice and procedures, collective bargaining on terms and conditions of employment, 'closed shop' agreements and arrangements.

Industrial Tribunals
The growth of industrial relations activity has resulted in a corresponding increase in the work of Industrial Tribunals which deal with complaints made by workers alleging infringement of their legal rights.

In setting up the tribunals, the government has taken care to ensure that like ACAS they are entirely independent. Indeed, they must be, since they are for practical purposes a court of law. A tribunal has three members only—a chairman who is legally qualified, one lay member drawn from a panel of nominees by management—usually the CBI—and another lay member chosen from a similar panel by the various trade unions. The proceedings are kept as informal as possible, although the rules of evidence, as in court, prevail. Each side is given the opportunity to state its case, calling witnesses if desired—again as in court—and may do this in person or by a representative. The tribunal considers the points made by both sides and, after retiring to consider its verdict, the chairman states what has been decided, often adding the reasons. The verdict is binding on both sides, but there is usually a right of appeal to the Employment Appeal Tribunal, somewhat similar to the Appeal Court in civil cases. Hearings usually take place in venues convenient to the employee.

At the outset of the case, that is, when the employee first brings the complaint, both he and the employer are required to submit their respective statements. Copies of these are exchanged between the parties, and, where appropriate, their representatives. At this stage either party may call in a conciliation officer from ACAS, who will, if agreed by both parties, bring them together. This procedure may be protracted since it may involve discussions with each side separately, but in most cases it avoids a tribunal hearing. Sometimes a settlement is agreed; in other cases the employee decides to withdraw the complaint. It should be emphasised, however, that the role of the ACAS officer is restricted to conciliation only; he cannot impose a settlement or decision on either party.

Collective Bargaining

Within the spirit of good industrial relations it is obviously desirable that general terms and conditions of employment in a firm should be acceptable both to management and workers. It is usual, therefore, to enter into 'collective bargaining'. This means setting up an arrangement, under which negotiations on behalf of the workers in a firm can take place. In a large firm such an arrangement may have to be divided into various sections or departments. When negotiations have been organised on these lines, a 'bargaining unit' is jointly created, by management and labour.

Workers' interests in such negotiations are usually handled by an appropriate trade union. The union may request 'recognition' for negotiation purposes, but the question of whether or not the union is recognised has to be decided by the employer, the employees and the trade union concerned; there is no legal obligation.

Trade Unions

Trade unions play a large part in the general field of industrial relations, and frequently their activities and those of their leaders feature in the press and other media. So it is appropriate in this context to note some of the features of trade unions generally.

Origin

From the mid-nineteenth century trade unions have been formed with the prime aim of promoting the well-being and protection of their members. This initially covered sickness and disablement benefit schemes, death benefits and assistance from benevolent funds; it moved on gradually to trade training and education. The unions had the nature of a brotherhood; local branches became known as 'Lodges,' and, in the printing industry, as 'Chapels'.

Purpose

As industrial relations have gained in importance the unions' predominant purpose has been to take part in negotiations with employers, employers' organisations and sometimes the government. Issues discussed include terms and conditions of employment, and sometimes trade disputes. To that end, unions use their strength and prestige. They act independently or in collaboration with the TUC, and make considerable use of ACAS facilities.

Many of the very large unions sponsor Members of Parliament, and successive governments have accepted unions as an effective means of joint consultation in the continuous growth of the industrial relations activity. The officers and general secretaries of some large unions become well-known national personalities as a result of the publicity given to their union work.

Organisation

Trade Unions are required to register under Friendly Society law, and to submit annual returns of membership statistics and finances to the Registrar of Friendly Societies. They are completely self-governing, and each has a constitution enabling members to elect, in a democratic manner, the officers, Executive Committee (or Council or similar title) and in many cases the General Secretatry. With a head office, and sometimes regional offices, the membership is arranged in geographical branches or sections; those in close proximity to each other often act on a regional basis.

Types of Union
There are three main types of union which can be summarised briefly as follows:

Craft Membership confined to a skilled occupation, such as the printing industry

Industrial Membership consisting of workers in a specific industry, irrespective of their individual occupations; the railway industry is an example

General Membership not restricted to any specific skill or trade, and therefore likely to be much larger than the other two types—e.g. the Transport and General Workers' Union

Closed Shop
This subject often features in trade union activity and it is helpful to have a general understanding of what the term means.

A closed shop can best be described as an agreement between an employer and one or more trade unions, requiring certain employees to be members of a trade union. The agreement need not be a formal one in writing, for it is often one which comes from custom and practice in the firm or trade.

The agreement does not necessarily require *all* employees in the firm to be members of the union, as particular classes of employees might be exempted. There is also provision in the Employment Act 1982 giving legal protection for those who do not want to belong to a trade union, but this is a complex subject outside the scope of this book and the student's immediate requirements.

The Trades Union Congress
The Trades Union Congress, established in 1868, is an association of trade unions which meets annually for one week as an assembly of delegates to discuss common problems, and to elect the governing body, the General Council.

The General Council monitors legislation, maintaining contact with Members of Parliament—both ministers and backbenchers—where necessary. It has a continuous relationship with all trade unions, the Confederation of British Industry (representing employers), and the many advisory and consultative bodies concerned with the various social and economic problems affecting the interests of workers and their unions, the majority of unions being affiliated to the TUC.

All affiliated unions are expected to notify the TUC of their claims for improvements in terms and conditions of employment. This enables the TUC Incomes Policy Committee to review them and advise unions.

The organisation of the TUC is under the control of the General Secretary, an Assistant General Secretary and staff of about 100 based in London, with some in the regions. There is an interesting range of departments, dealing with international trade unionism, research and economics, production, social insurance, welfare and education.

Employers' Associations

Just as workers have a representative body—the trade unions with the TUC—to protect their interests and negotiate on their behalf, so too have employers. Throughout industry and commerce there is a wide range of employers' associations, comparable with the range of trade unions.

Largest and most important among these is the Confederation of British Industry (the CBI), recognised by the government, and the unions as the leading body that speaks for employers.

The CBI is well organised and has a very influential membership, electing, in a democratic manner, its officers and governing committee. It has its headquarters in London and offices in the regions.

The principal industrial and commercial employers also have representation through employers' associations, some frequently in the news, and consequently well-known. The Engineering Employers' Federation, the Newspaper Publishers' Association, the Food Manufacturers' Federation, the Road Haulage Association are among these.

There are also some voluntary associations in the business world which do not participate in industrial relations work, but undertake other useful services, such as research, international links, publications, information and advice. These include professional institutions, such as the British Standards Institution, the Institute of Export, the Industrial Society, the Institute of Personnel Management, the Institute of Chartered Secretaries and Administrators, the Institute of Chartered Accountants, and the Chambers of Commerce, of which the London Chamber of Commerce and Industry is an outstanding example.

23

THE HUMAN ELEMENT

The relationship between master and servant, employer and employee, manager and worker—any situation where one serves another for reward—involves the human element.

No matter how much automation, machinery or modern equipment is introduced, and no matter what the distance is between the parties, the human element plays an indispensable part.

Whatever the personal status, everyone on both sides is human, with all the frailties, failings—and skills—which are part of the individual's make-up. So, it must be recognised, industrial psychology is of vital importance to everyone.

There are various definitions and interpretations of industrial psychology, but probably the most acceptable is: 'The application of psychological methods and results to problems arising in the industrial and commercial field, including the selection of workers, their training, and the methods and conditions of employment.'

With that definition in mind, and proceeding step by step, it is interesting to see the stages through which an employee may pass, and how these stages involve the employer or manager.

Basic aims—management and labour

Management aims. A flow of production of constant quality; the freedom to transfer employees to other work at short notice in unforeseen contingencies; strong loyalty of employees, and economic cost consistent with reliability and quality of products.

Labour aims. Adequate remuneration with definite prospects of advancement in status and pay; security and pension rights, good working conditions with fringe benefits, and the feeling of pride in 'belonging to the firm'.

If these aims can be achieved by both sides there can be a partnership between management and labour which will give profitable productivity and a sense of security and prosperity to all concerned.

Recruitment and selection

Many sources of worker recruitment exist and cater for differing requirements, depending on the status and requirements of the position to be filled. The Manpower Services Commission of the Department of Employment operates the Job Centres which are found in most town centres. These offer a comprehensive service in bringing together employers and job-seekers. Job Centres do not deal solely with the unemployed, but offer the same service to people who are employed but want a change, or progress in their career. Vacancies handled by the centres relate to full-time, temporary and part-time work in every section of industry and commerce.

Other sources of recruitment are:

	Type of work
School-leavers	Trainee or junior posts
University graduates	Semi-senior grades
Recruitment bodies	
Professional and Executive Register (PER), Department of Employment;	Senior Executives
Professional bodies and trade unions;	Appointments requiring special skills and/or professional qualifications
Employment consultants;	Appropriate appointments of a varied nature
Advertising in national local and trade press;	As above
Professional journals	Suitably qualified staff for the relevant professions

Note: In all recruitment it is essential to comply with the requirements of the Sex Discrimination, Equal Pay and Race Relations Acts. (See page 204)

The selection of applicants to fill the vacancies must be done with the greatest possible care. The cost of recruiting, advertising, interviewing, etc., is an unavoidable expense, but it is wasted if the applicant selected and appointed is found soon afterwards to be unsuitable for the work. Successful selection is an art in itself, since it usually has to be based on reactions at the final interview. It is absolutely essential, therefore, to have a carefully designed form for issue to applicants. The information given on the application form, and sometimes the way in which it is filled in, can be of great help in deciding on the selection—and also in the earlier decision of inviting an applicant for interview.

Conditions of service

Having taken the selection decision, the next logical step is to agree with the applicant the conditions of service, that is, the terms and conditions under which he or she will work. The Employment Protection (Consolidation) Act stipulates that within thirteen weeks of starting work the employer must give the employee a 'written statement' of terms and conditions. In practice, however, this is too long an interval, and it may be mutually convenient to hand or send the statement to the successful applicant when he or she accepts the job offered.

In addition to basic information on pay, holidays, notice for termination and title of job, the statement must contain details of what is known as the grievance procedure. This must give the name or description of the person to whom the employee should go with any grievance relating to the work, or any matter concerned with discipline.

In practice, most firms set out all the points mentioned above on a printed form, to be completed only with names, dates, amounts, etc. relevant to the applicant. It may of course, be convenient to the firm to include in the 'statement' other appropriate details, such as trade union membership, staff pensions scheme, welfare facilities and so on.

Induction procedure

A very important part of the process of giving a new employee the 'sense of belonging' to a firm, is a carefully planned induction. A senior employee, usually a member of the personnel department, ensures that the employee is fully briefed about the firm and the nature of the job.

There should first be a tour of the work-place, with introductions to the appropriate members of staff or workers, the supervisors, and a description of *their* job, to show how it fits in with that to be done by the newly-engaged person. He or she should be shown the location of the canteen, toilets, rest-room, cloakroom, lockers, fire exits, car or cycle parks, and prohibited areas.

After this there would normally be a short talk explaining particular aspects of the job, including items such as basic pay and overtime; bonus pay or commission; holiday and sick pay; method of pay, showing how the pay slip is made up; pension scheme contributions; time-keeping records; disciplinary and grievance procedures as in the statement of conditions of service; operation of the Statutory Sick Pay scheme; safety at work regulations, including fire drill.

Pay and fringe benefits

Pay

The rate of pay offered and accepted on engagement must be set out in an 'itemised pay statement' to comply with the Employment Protection (Consolidation) Act 1978, as amended by the Employment Act 1982. The statement is usually held to be the wage or salary slip; a printed form is usually standard in the wages department. It must be given or sent to the employee, either with the payment of wages or salary, or before payment. The following details must appear:

(a) Gross amount of wages or salary, and other earnings
(b) Amount of deductions for such items as income tax under the PAYE system; National Insurance contributions; staff pension scheme contributions (if any); any other fixed amounts agreed in advance, such as trade union subscriptions, National Saving Scheme payments
(c) Net amount of wages or salary payable

If the payment is made in cash it would be useful for the pay statement to be included with the cash. If payment is made by bank transfer to the employee's account the statement would be issued shortly before the transfer was made.

Incentive schemes

There are advantages to firms in introducing wage incentive schemes. Employees are rewarded for increased output and/or reducing production costs. Schemes on these lines have various titles—merit awards, performance payments, piece-work payments, etc., but all have the same aim—a benefit to both management and labour. Other forms of incentive include commission on individual sales performance in a given period, and bonus on a department's annual or quarterly financial results.

Fringe benefits

These may vary greatly according to the nature and size of the firm, and may include such items as: subsidised meals in the staff restaurant or canteen; luncheon vouchers; free or concessionary use of the firm's facilities, discount on purchases of the firm's products, use of a company car by certain categories of employee.

Pension schemes

National Health Insurance contributions paid by all employees include a payment to the state pension scheme and this, together with payments made by the employer, provides a state-funded retirement pension based on earnings.

Many employers, and almost all large companies operate a staff pension scheme. This is regarded as an important asset to the company's good relations with employees and it encourages long service. The scheme may be self-financing with very large companies, or—more usual—financed through one of the large life insurance companies. Employer and employee both pay into the scheme; the employee's contribution is usually 5 per cent of earnings. Depending on salary and length of service this type of scheme may provide a substantial pension.

Fair treatment

In all matters involving the human element the greatest requirement is fairness. Fair play is always welcomed, especially so in employee relations. Good employers seek to keep their work force intact, to maintain good productivity and avoid the expenses of recruitment. So they encourage long service by good working conditions, progressive pay schemes, good promotion prospects, pension scheme and fringe benefits.

Good employers will also develop 'job satisfaction', or motivation, amongst their employees. A happy and contented work force gives of its best to the benefit of all concerned.

Communication

Good communication is vital, and should take the form of joint consultation on aspects of the business where staff discussion can play a useful part.

Ideally, joint consultation should have full managerial support, making available information on the firm's financial position in trading, future prospects for trade, and future policy on new developments. There should be frequent and well-attended meetings between management and staff where both are equally represented. The meetings should be properly constituted, with agenda, efficient chairmanship, secretarial arrangements and adequate reports to the work force. The agenda should include submissions from both sides, sent in well in advance of the meetings. It follows that, from the management or staff, there could be considered submissions on any proposed change in terms and conditions of employment, etc., leading to an amicable and fair decision.

Equal Opportunity, Sex Discrimination and Racial Equality

Bearing in mind the spirit of fairness, great care must be taken in regard to the Equal Pay Act 1970, the Sex Discrimination Act 1975, and the Race Relations Act 1976. This is complex law, but in simple terms it provides that all shall be regarded and respected on equal terms, and available for employment in almost any kind of work, subject only to their ability and efficiency. Any person who considers that his or her rights under this legislation have been disregarded may take the complaint to an Industrial Tribunal.

Grievance procedure. If any employee has a grievance relating to his or her work, that employee is entitled to have the matter fairly investigated by a definite procedure which exists for the purpose. The statement of conditions of service, issued to the employee on engagement, specified the person to whom the grievance must first be taken. That person will have some authority to ensure that the case is fairly dealt with, to the satisfaction of all concerned. (Note should be taken of the ACAS Code of Practice on this subject.)

Termination of employment. The need for fairness, as described earlier in this chapter, continues right up to the end of employment. When dismissing an employee, the employer must ensure that the reasons for the dismissal are fair in all respects; otherwise the employee could, after a minimum of one year with the firm, complain to the Industrial Tribunal, claiming compensation for unfair dismissal. (If the employer is a small firm with a maximum of 20 employees, the minimum period of one year in work is extended to two years.) The dismissed worker also has the right to receive, on request, a statement of the reasons for dismissal.

Redundancy. The same principle of fairness applies to the end of employment because of redundancy. The employer must ensure that the persons made redundant were chosen fairly, not out of turn, on the normal principle of 'last in first out'. An aggrieved employee could take a case of this kind to the Industrial Tribunal in the same manner as one for unfair dismissal.

Notice to terminate.   It is obviously necessary to give reasonable notice to terminate employment, and the statement of conditions of employment will usually specify the periods of notice to be given. Employment law sets down a minimum period of one week for employment which has continued for at least one month but less than two years; for employment over two years, but less than twelve years, the notice required is one week for each year worked; and for work of more than twelve years' duration the notice is twelve weeks. These periods of notice are essentially the minimum which employers are required to give and it may be that in the conditions of service statement—or a contract, in the case of senior staff—longer periods would be stated, and would, of course, apply. The minimum notice to be given by an employee is one week, after a month's work, but the terms of engagement may require a longer period.

Industrial training

The need for training.   This continues throughout employment at most levels; for many the need is constant because of the progressive introduction of new methods, techniques and skills.

School leavers, in their career preparation, have an obvious need for further education and training. Their educational attainments, coupled with their inherent natural abilities should be linked to modern methods of training, to fit them for the most appropriate kind of work. In this way they are helped to overcome the problems, often acute, of taking the first step along their career.

New employees, including school leavers, have a pressing need to acquire new abilities and skills with which to obtain 'job satisfaction' for themselves and become increasingly valuable to their new employers.

Semi-senior and supervisory staff may have sufficient service and skill to merit training for further advancement with the firm, possibly with the object of the professional qualification appropriate to their work.

Senior and management staff could benefit from the specialised short courses available in a variety of management and technical fields; such courses exist at the business schools linked to the Universities of London, Manchester, etc. In all this there is a growing recognition by many firms of the great value of effective training of staff, on whom the future success of the firm may well depend.

Sources of training.   Taken in a logical sequence, the main sources and types of training commence with that for young people, referred to above. For those who have not taken their first job since leaving school, the government has a special responsibility. This is seen in the considerable organisation of the Youth Training Scheme, described below.

For those already in their first job, many firms provide their own inside training, and in that connection the Industrial Training Boards, which operate in some trades, provide financial and practical assistance. New workers are encouraged by some firms to take day-release courses, in suitable skills relating to their work, at local technical colleges and polytechnics.

Higher education at colleges is offered for the examinations of the various professional and other bodies, and many employers encourage their staff to obtain relevant qualifications, by such means as financial assistance for books and fees, and by permitting attendance at daytime classes, etc.

Correspondence courses for professional bodies' examinations provide an acceptable alternative for those who have no local college offering courses, and these are also encouraged by many employers, as are some commercial colleges which offer specialised courses in such subjects as marketing, salesmanship, computers, languages, etc. University studies represent the highest point of most training and take the form of degree courses, and also a growing number of post-graduate courses.

In training there must always be an advantage to all concerned, because there is a lasting gain both to management and labour. The community must also benefit from the good service and efficiency that results from well trained and qualified people conducting the nation's business.

Youth Training Scheme.   This scheme is organised by the Manpower Services Commission of the Department of Employment. It provides training places for sixteen-year-old school leavers, both employed and unemployed, and some seventeen-year-old unemployed school leavers.

A two-year-long programme of planned work-experience is linked with work-related training or further education at college. The scheme is designed for young people of all abilities and aims to help them acquire skills and experience to enhance their careers.

The scheme is supported by a great amount of goodwill on the part of employers, trade unions, and education authorities. At national level the whole scheme is supervised by a Youth Training Board, comprising employers, trade unions, local authorities, education authorities, voluntary and youth organisations. It is also assisted by a professional group which advises on standards and content of training. The ultimate aim of the scheme is to provide the nation with the skilled work-force of the future.

TEST QUESTIONS ━━━━━━━━━━━━━━━━━━━━━

These questions from the 'Structure of Business' papers of past years are made available by courtesy of the London Chamber of Commerce Education Scheme. They are grouped according to topics.

In recent years the London Chamber of Commerce has developed two levels of this examination—The Private Secretary's Certificate (PSC) and the Secretarial Studies Certificate (SSC). In addition the examiner asks pertinent questions on what could be termed current affairs in business. Such questions are necessarily ephemeral and date quickly. They have not been included here, but teachers in particular would be well advised to obtain sets of papers from the London Chamber of Commerce, Marlowe House, 109 Station Road, Sidcup, Kent, in order to acquaint themselves with the style of these questions.

Government departments and local government

1. What are the objectives of central government in managing the state of the economy? Do any of the objectives conflict with one another?

2. With reference to your own country outline the role of government in encouraging training for work.

3. Describe clearly the ways in which business activity may be affected by your government's fiscal policy.

4. *Either*
   (*a*) Explain the relevance to the business community of the following government departments:
   (i)   The Treasury;
   (ii) Export Credit Guarantee Department;
   (iii) The Central Office of Information.

   Or
   (*b*) Selecting examples drawn from your own country, explain how

the process of exporting may be aided by both governmental and non-governmental bodies.

5. Describe the major functions and services of any one local authority. Answer with particular reference to its influence upon business.

6. (a) As Chairman of the Metropolitan District Council you have received a letter from a local businessman complaining about the latest rise in rates. Compose a suitable letter in reply, identifying those services provided which you believe to be of particular benefit in the local community.

   Overseas-based candidates may answer (b) as an alternative

   (b) Write a letter to the London Chamber of Commerce and Industry from the head office of your organisation (which is registered outside the UK) explaining the services provided locally by your government which are of benefit to businessmen.

7. Select *one* tier of local government organisation, outline its structure, and explain the influence it could have upon the business community.

8. Why is a central government concerned with the balance of payments for its country? What steps does it take to attempt to improve the balance of payments position?

9. *Either*
   (a) Why do the majority of governments wish to control inflation? What measures may be used to control it?

   Or
   (b) In simple terms explain what you understand by the 'balance of payments'. Explain briefly how the following developments might affect a country's balance of payments:
      (i) a rise in the price of home-manufactured consumer goods;
      (ii) the removal of tariff barriers as a result of joining a trading block (e.g. European Economic Community).

10. With reference to your own country, outline in general terms the extent of inflation and the measures being taken in an effort to control it.

11. (a) Explain the relevance to the business community of the following government departments:
    (i)   Department of Transport;
    (ii) The Treasury;
    (iii) The Commissioners of Inland Revenue.

    Or

    (b) Selecting examples drawn from your own country, outline the various ways in which central government may influence industry and commerce.

12. Select four of the following pairs and explain the difference in meaning:
    (a) standard of living : cost of living
    (b) deflation   : devaluation
    (c) tariff   : quota
    (d) mixed economy   : mixed enterprise
    (e) job analysis   : job specification

13. What is the value of international trade both to a country as a whole and to the individual inhabitants?

14. Outline the work of the main organisations concerned with the selling and arrangement for shipment of exports.

15. Give reasons why countries participate in international trading. What artificial barriers to such trade may be imposed by central government?

16. Should Britain remain a member of the European Community (Common Market)? State the reasons for your opinion.

17. Do you consider that United Kingdom industry has benefited from membership of the European Economic Community? Give reasons for your answer.

Public and private sector business organisations

18. What advantages are to be gained by a sole proprietor who decides to convert his enterprise into a partnership? Are there any consequent disadvantages?

19. Three of your friends have decided to go into business together providing a typing and secretarial service for small firms. They are undecided on what form of business should be set up and have come to you for advice. What would you suggest and why?

20. *Either*
    (a) Explain the organisation and different roles of the following co-operative business units:
       (i)   retail co-operatives;
       (ii) producers' co-operatives;
       (iii) Co-operative Wholesale Society.

    Or
    (b) Assume that you have to advise your employer, who is a sole proprietor, on the benefits and possible disadvantages of converting his business to a private joint-stock company. Outline the major factors which you would mention.

21. 'Delegation is the passing on of responsibility'.
    What do you understand by this statement? Support your answer by choosing one form of business unit and explaining how delegation might operate within it.

22. Compare and contrast the duties and obligations of a board of directors in a public limited company with that of its shareholders and salaried managers.

23. What are the major sources of finance available to a multi-national company?

24. Your employer, a manufacturing company, is undertaking two extra projects:
    (a) to develop a new factory in a depressed area;
    (b) a special order which will be completed within two years.
    Both will involve an extra investment in machines, material and labour. What sources of finance could you recommend for each of these projects?

25. *Either*
    (a) Choosing one major public corporation, outline the reasons for its creation and explain its present structure.

Or

(b) Explain the term 'public ownership', giving an outline of its pattern in your own country.

26. Selecting examples drawn from your own country, outline the extent to which the government is involved in the economy through public enterprise undertakings.

27. Outline the major differences between the public joint stock company and the public corporation. Refer in your answer to the pattern of organisation and control and to the financial structure.

Commercial services

28. What are the functions of a central bank? Answer, with reference to your own country.

29. In what ways does a central bank differ from a commercial bank?

30. What role do the commercial banks play in the encouragement of industrial and economic growth?

31. What services do the commercial banks and merchant banks offer in relation to the provision of capital for manufacturing industry?

32. How is the operation of a stock exchange linked to the activities of a public joint-stock company and of central government?

33. 'A stock exchange is a market for the buying and selling of shares'. Does such a definition, in your view, adequately explain the role of the stock exchange? Answer by reference to the functions of a stock exchange.

34. Briefly explain the major principles underlying insurance contracts. Select four classes of insurance and explain why these would be beneficial to a self-employed builder who has two assistants.

35. Given the following business transactions, outline the types of insurance likely to be required:

(i) the sale of furniture by a manufacturer in a major city, to a large retail organisation with branches throughout the country;

(ii) the sale of heavy machinery by a Scottish-based company, to an engineering company in Germany.

36. Briefly outline the types of insurance which would particularly interest the following business organisations:

(i) A sole proprietor owning a single 'corner shop';

(ii) A public joint-stock company operating an international passenger airline fleet;

(iii) A medium-sized manufacturing company producing garden and agricultural chemicals and fertilisers.

Trade unions; Industrial relations; Industrial psychology; Living standards

37. What role is played by trade unions in the field of industrial relations?

38. What do you understand by the term 'industrial relations'? What is the role of the trade union movement in this field?

39. How do you think a good working relationship between management and employees can be established and maintained?

40. Why is it important that the potential private secretary should have a basic knowledge of industrial psychology?

41. Briefly outline the areas covered by a study of industrial psychology. How are job satisfaction and motivation to work related to each other?

42. Why should the manager be concerned with such factors as leadership and motivation when seeking to encourage productivity? Do not limit your answer to the two elements of industrial psychology mentioned.

43. Explain the different wage payment systems which you would expect to find in operation within both the private and public sectors.

44. How are wages determined within the private sector? How can wage levels be influenced by central government?

45. What do you understand by the term 'incomes policy'? Suggest reasons why such a policy would be introduced and mention some of its possible effects.

46. What do you understand by the term 'standard of living'? How may central government influence the economic well-being of its people?

47. Explain the relationship between the state of the 'national economy' and the 'standard of living' in your country.

Miscellaneous

48. Outline the major functions and relationships with the business community of *two* of the following:
    (a) advertising agencies;
    (b) management consultants;
    (c) market research companies.

49. Answer *two* of the following.
    Describe briefly the differences between:
    (a) joint-stock bank and merchant bank;
    (b) chambers of commerce and trade associations;
    (c) insurance broker and underwriter;
    (d) profit and non-profit making organisations.

50. Write a short account of the work and importance of *two* of the following:
    (a) a trade association;
    (b) consumer protection organisations;
    (c) a chamber of commerce;
    (d) the Confederation of British Industry.

51. Select *four* of the following pairs and explain the difference in meaning:
    (a) national income   :   national debt
    (b) balance of trade   :   balance of payments

(c) debenture   :   share
(d) direct taxation :   indirect taxation
(e) sales department :   marketing department

52. Explain the general principles of insurance operation by reference to each of the following related terms:
   (i)   insurable interest;
   (ii) utmost good faith;
   (iii) indemnity;
   (iv) contribution and subrogation.

53. Briefly explain the following terms which are used in the study of industrial psychology:
   (i)   job satisfaction;
   (ii) leadership;
   (iii) attitudes;
   (iv) communications.

Departments of a business and their relationship with each other

54. Factory workers often regard the office services of a company as unproductive. Show how good office administration contributes to higher productivity and profits, and to the competitiveness of the company's products.

55. What are the functions of a managing director in relation to the shareholders and the board, and in the day-to-day operations of his company?

56. Describe the work of *either:* a chief accountant and his department, *or* a borough treasurer and his department.

57. Very large sums of money are spent annually on advertising and sales promotion in the United Kingdom. What does industry and commerce expect from this large expenditure and how can it be justified?

58. A company contemplates opening an additional factory. What departments would be most affected by such a step, and who should be consulted regarding the size and location of the new factory?

59. In today's highly competitive situation at home and abroad, many companies have put greater emphasis on their sales activities, and marketing departments have been formed. Describe the range of activities that could take place in such a marketing department.

60. Discuss some of the methods of management a firm can use to communicate with the workers.

61. Put forward the arguments of 'promoting from within' and 'recruiting from outside'.

62. Which departments within a large industrial organisation are responsible for controlling costs, and how is such control effected?

63. Outline the role of research, design and development within a manufacturing enterprise.

64. In what ways can the personnel department be particularly useful to the production department?

65. What is the function of marketing within a large manufacturing company? Outline the contacts which would take place between the marketing department and other departments.

66. Select *two* important departments which you would expect to find in a large public joint-stock company, and explain the interrelationships which exist between them.

67. Describe and explain the main features of a system of production control within a private enterprise manufacturing company.

68. Identify and describe *three* types of production system. Why may more than one type exist within the same industry?

69. What steps may a Marketing Department take to ensure successful new product development?

70. How does the process of production planning and control aid the flow of high quality products?

INDEX